A Working Manual for

Altar Guilds

A Working Manual for

Altar Guilds

Third Edition

by Dorothy C. Diggs

MOREHOUSE PUBLISHING
A Continuum imprint
HARRISBURG • LONDON • NEW YORK

Morehouse Publishing
P.O. Box 1321
Harrisburg, PA 17105

Morehouse Publishing is a Continuum imprint.

Library of Congress Cataloging-in-Publication Data

Diggs, Dorothy C.
    A working manual for altar guilds / by Dorothy C.
Diggs—3rd ed.

    p.   cm.
ISBN 0-8192-1455-8

    1. Altar guilds—Episcopal Church-Handbooks, manuals, etc.
2. Episcopal Church—Liturgy—Handbooks, manuals, etc.
3. Anglican Communion—Liturgy—Handbooks, manuals, etc.
I. Title
BX5948.D54   1988   247—dc19   87-31238   CIP

Library of Congress Catalog Card Number 57-6108

Printed in the United States of America

07 06 05 04   10 9 8 7

To

THE REVEREND JOHN HEUSS, D.D.
*Late Rector of the Parish of Trinity Church
New York City*

FOREWORD

* * * * *

Ministry manifests itself in many different ways within the life of the Church. The ministry of the Altar Guild is one which is sometimes forgotten because of the dedication of its membership. It is assumed that either the members need no nurturing or no new members are needed. But this ministry, like all other ministries of the Body of Christ, needs to be nurtured and empowered.

This book provides the Church with a means by which persons called to a ministry of service as members of the Altar Guild might be nurtured in and empowered for this ministry. For both the seasoned veteran and the neophyte, these detailed descriptions will provide the approach for strengthening their ministry within the life of the congregation.

I hope that members of the Altar Guilds will also nurture their spiritual lives as they serve the Church. This book provides many "how to's," but the ministry must be grounded in faith and in our baptisms.

Edmond L. Browning
Presiding Bishop

Prayer for Fidelity

Teach us, Good Lord, to serve Thee as Thou
deservest—
To give and not to count the cost,
To fight and not to heed the wounds,
To toil and not to seek for rest,
To labor and not to ask for any reward save that of
    knowing that we do
Thy will, Through Jesus Christ, our Lord.

Amen.

PREFACE

to the

Revised Edition

In the early days of the Church the duty of caring for the altar and sanctuary was the concern of the priests and attendants. Nuns do this work now in certain parts of the world, but, for some years, in most churches, these duties have been performed by a specially chosen group of women known as the Altar Guild or Chapter.

It is not known just when the transition from priests and helpers took place. As Altar Guild work is a housekeeping service, it probably developed when the clergy became too busy spreading the Good News to continue it. As a precedent, we are told that in our Lord's time "faithful women ministered to Him." It is certain that He elevated the position of women to a dignity they had not known before.

There are legends as to the patron saint of Altar Guilds. St. Monica, for the simplicity of her life and her dedication to Christianity, St. Agatha of Sicily, martyred for her faith, St. Martha of Bethany, for her practical life of active service, and St. Anne, mother of the Blessed Virgin Mary, are among those mentioned.

Women aspiring to become members of an Altar Guild should be well-informed communicants. The work can be done with more dedication and intelligence if those engaged in it are thoroughly familiar with the Book of Common Prayer, the changing seasons of the Church year, the names of the sections of the church building, and can identify everything used in the sanctuary and sacristy.

Since the revision of the Book of Common Prayer in 1979, there has been increased congregational participation in the worship of the Church. Women are also discovering new roles within our liturgical practices as they are being incorporated into the total life of the Church.

For Altar Guilds, the changing styles of architecture in the churches, built without chancels and with freestanding altars, should be of particular interest. The duties of the Altar Guild, however, remain the same. Because of varying degrees of ceremonial in the parishes and missions of the Episcopal Church the service may range from very simple to very elaborate. But in every case, the objective is care, beauty, and traditional correctness attendant upon the worship of Almighty God.

From our missions where facilities may be limited, to the churches of our cities having the best vesture, the impression created must be of handiwork done with loving care and offered to God's glory as the best effort of his handmaidens and housekeepers.

There are excellent books obtainable on the making of vestments, the symbolism of our matchless liturgy, the special care of vestments and vessels and the best materials and metals to be used. These things will not be covered here except when relevant. We will try to set forth a pattern of preparation which may be used in any Episcopal Church. Churches having less than the stipulated equipment may simplify it to their need. Churches having a more elaborate ceremonial may wish to add to it. In the latter case the officiating clergy will know the setting they want and can instruct the members of the Altar Guild in its preparation.

The author owes a great debt to the late Rev. Dr. John Heuss whose inspired leadership was responsible for many years of rewarding service.

Grateful thanks are due to the Rt. Rev. Wallace E. Conkling, to the Rev. Canon Royden Keith Yerkes, and to the Rev. Dr. Allen Brown, Jr. for reading the manuscript and making important and helpful changes. Also to the Rev. Dr. William H. Anthony for a lifetime of instruction in the ways and teachings of the Church. Thanks are also due to Mrs. Betty S. K. Wolfe, who made the line drawings of the symbols.

It must ever be borne in mind that the mechanics of preparation here set forth are but the means to an end and not the end itself—which is the glory of God, full of grace and truth.   D.C.D.

Fort Myers, Florida
June, 1987

CONTENTS

A Working Manual
for
Altar Guilds

1

The Services

*****

THE ALTAR

In recent years there have been radical changes in church architecture and with them have come new settings and placement of the altar. The design with which we were once familiar is the traditional church built in a cruciform shape with the altar against the east wall on a foot-pace and steps leading up to it. The communion rail separates it from the choir within the chancel, from which more steps lead down into the nave. Since some Episcopal churches still follow this pattern, most of the instructions here can be followed by them.

In building churches today the trend is to a modern design with free-standing altar in a sanctuary enclosed by the communion rail and with the nave directly adjoining—that is, without the customary choir and chancel. The choir is usually in a balcony at the rear of the church and the offices are all said in the sanctuary. Churches which have a chapel often say the Daily Offices there. Week-day celebrations of the Holy Communion as well as occasional services are also said in the Chapel.

A number of new churches now have an "altar in the round." The altar is on a platform in the center of the sanctuary, surrounded by the communion rail, and the pews are in a circle outside this. Such an altar presents a different approach in preparing for the services.

1

The altar is the center of the Church's life and is the major concern of Altar Guilds. It should be vested with the greatest care and always kept in immaculate condition. By ancient custom the standard vestments of the Altar are, in this order: cerecloth, frontal and fair linen. To these may be added whatever is needed for any particular service. Instead of a frontal, some churches use a superfrontal, which is shorter and may be of the season color or simply of lace. (Lace should not be used during Advent and Lent.) Some use a frontal with superfrontal as well.

The white altar coverings should be made of linen, if possible, although synthetic materials are now often used. What the 1979 Prayer Book calls "a clean, white cloth" we have always known as "the fair linen." The fair linen is the "fair white linen cloth" required by Prayer Book rubric. It should hang at least eighteen inches at the ends of the altar. On a solid stone or wood altar, it may hang to within a few inches of the floor. It should not touch the floor. If the altar is a table type with a recessed foundation, the fair linen should not hand much, if any, longer than eighteen inches or it will tend to ripple. Common sense should determine which length is most suitable for any particular altar.

Except when preparing for the Holy Communion, the fair linen should always be covered. If any service other than the Holy Communion is to take place, a white cloth should be put upon the fair linen, which for want of a better term may be called a prayer cover or prayer cloth. This is a white linen cloth which exactly fits the mensa, or top of the altar, and does not have ends overhanging. The reason for this cloth is that the fair linen will not long remain either "fair" or "white" if constantly exposed.

When the altar is in repose between services, it should be covered by a dust protector. This protector should completely cover the top of the altar and hang over the ends to the edge of the fair linen. It may be of virgin blue, green, or dark red, with a simple cross upon it to denote its sacred use, or it may be quite elaborate, made of a rich material with embroidery, if desired. If frontals in the colors of the Church seasons are used, a dust cover which harmonizes with these might be chosen.

There can be a difference between a free-standing altar and an altar standing free so that one may walk behind it. With either there will have to be a flexible approach to vesting it. If the altar stands out from the wall so that the priest may celebrate facing the people, the usual frontal or super-frontal may still be usable. If celebrating behind the altar is a new procedure and the six office candles have previously been used, they will have to be dispensed with. Some churches are designed with gradines or re-tables in or under the reredos. The office candles might be put there as well as the flowers. If not, the design of the sanctuary will determine what is to be done about flowers as well as the necessary adjuncts to the services.

For an "altar-in-the-round" or one on a platform on the nave floor, the traditional frontal can hardly be used. The frontal could be omitted entirely and the altar vested simply in cerecloth and fair linen with the two candlesticks. For this type of altar a Jacobean frontal, or a modified version of it, could be used. This covers the altar on all sides and hangs to the floor. Care must be taken not to use too heavy material or make the frontal too full lest it bunch up at the ends and possibly get in the way of the officiants at services.

With the coming of the new Prayer Book there has been a number of changes in procedure. Each parish priest will decide what is best for that particular congregation. Altar Guild members will follow instructions and be helpful and cooperative in order that the transition from the customary Prayer Book rite may be as easy as possible for clergy and people.

MORNING AND EVENING PRAYER
Morning and Evening Prayer are choir offices, which means they were said in the choir, not in the sanctuary. This is not possible now except in traditional churches. The altar is cov-

ered with the prayer cloth over its standard vestments. Nothing else need be upon it.

When there are two gradines or retables behind the altar, the cross and candlesticks may be upon the upper retable.

Flowers in appropriate color for the Church season should be carefully arranged and put upon the lower retable. Some churches have niches for flowers at the sides of the altar—others use stands. Some have corbels (see definitions, page 110).

The candles must stand straight in their sticks and be as nearly the same height as possible. As they burn down, the tallest should be put next to the cross and the rest graded proportionately down.

If the church has an altar without retables, the candle sticks and flowers can be put along the back of the altar itself.

Alms basins are placed on or under the credence table, or perhaps in a wall niche.

For Morning and Evening Prayer the clergy are normally vested in cassock and surplice with tippet, and academic hoods if desired. Some priests wear stoles in place of tippets, especially if they are preaching. Stoles, if worn, should be the color of the Church season.

The Bible marker and pulpit fall follow the color of the Church season. The altar service book is marked at places specified by the clergy.

Altar Guild members should arrive for duty at least a half hour before the service is to begin, in order not to be seen at work by the congregation. They should remain in the sacristy until the arrival of the clergy to carry out any requests or changes. They should not go into the sanctuary after the service is over until the congregation has left the church.

After the Morning or Evening Prayer service is concluded, the prayer cloth should be removed from the altar and the dust protector put upon it. The candles should be trimmed or straightened, if necessary, and the sanctuary carefully checked and made tidy. Kneeling cushions should be put straight and books closed.

The Bible usually stays permanently on the lectern and is left closed. Some ministers prefer the open Bible and have it left so at all times.

There should be a special box or bank bag in which to put the offerings after the service. Alms basins, if brass, should be kept in felt or flannel bags to protect the metal.

THE HOLY COMMUNION

For this primary service of the Church, the altar is vested in its standard coverings of cerecloth, frontal or superfrontal or both, and fair linen, spotlessly clean. This is the only service at which the fair linen is exposed, that is without a protecting prayer cloth. Upon the fair linen go the two eucharistic candlesticks. On a free-standing altar these are placed toward the front of the altar and equidistant from the ends.

The altar service book, or missal, upon the missal stand, is placed on the epistle side near the normal side for celebration. It should be marked with a ribbon, placed at the beginning of the communion service at locations specified by the clergy, and the book left closed.

Appropriate flowers should be carefully arranged in the vases or containers, brought to the altar and placed at one side, or on the retable, or in a suitable niche, according to the altar design.

If there are two credence tables, the offering plates are put upon the one on the gospel side of the altar. If there is but one credence table, it should be upon the epistle side of the altar and the alms basins may be put on the shelf underneath it or in a suitable niche.

On the epistle side credence table go the two cruets of wine and water, the wine customarily on the right, the water on the left with the handles facing rearwards. The bread box, with sufficient bread, is placed between them at the back, with the lavabo bowl and lavabo towel beside it at the left.

At an early celebration of the Holy Communion, the vested chalice may be put upon the altar and the corporal spread, or it may be put upon the credence and brought to the celebrant at the proper place in the service, usually by the acolyte. If a guest priest is celebrating, it is wise to ascertain beforehand just what the procedure will be because some priests prefer to carry the vested chalice to the altar themselves. When a bishop is the celebrant, the chalice should be put upon the altar before the service and the corporal spread. When the vested chalice is in the sacristy in readiness for a service, it

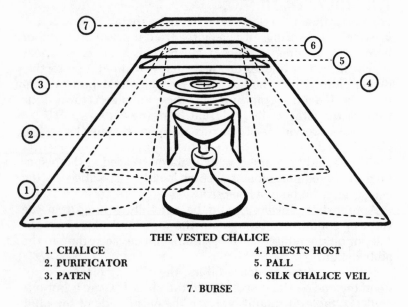

THE VESTED CHALICE

1. CHALICE   4. PRIEST'S HOST
2. PURIFICATOR   5. PALL
3. PATEN   6. SILK CHALICE VEIL
                7. BURSE

should be placed front in with the veil folded over it so that the priest may more readily grasp it.

If a second chalice is needed, it may be put on the credence and brought by the server to the celebrant before bringing the elements. In this case the veiled chalice should be put on the altar beforehand and the corporal spread. A pall and purificator must be provided for the second chalice.

On occasions when especially large congregations are being prepared for and third and fourth chalices needed, there may not be room for them on the credence. They may then be

SILK CHALICE VEIL

BURSE

placed on the altar in a row behind the veiled chalice and covered with palls or their own patens, or some with the one, some with the other. Lace veils are sometimes used for the supplementary chalices, but experience has proved palls more satisfactory, since there is always danger of the soft veil getting into the sacrament. For services where three or more chalices are used it is well to have a corporal large enough to accommodate all, perhaps thirty inches square. Whatever size, it must be made square. If none so large is immediately available, two smaller ones may be used in order that all chalices may rest upon them. Extra purificators must be provided for the chalices, and rather than having so many in the burse, it seems more convenient to put them to the right of the chalices on the fair linen, not on the corporal.

The burse, if used, stands to the side of the chalice and near one of the candlesticks.

It should be remembered, however, that "during the Great Thanksgiving it is appropriate that there be only one chalice on the Altar, and, if need be, a flagon of wine from which additional chalices may be filled after the Breaking of the Bread" (Prayer Book, p. 407).

The celebrant may wear a surplice and a stole in the color of the Church season, or eucharistic vestments if it is the custom. Eucharistic vestments are laid out in the sacristy. A white linen cloth should be put first on the table or vestment chest where the vestments are to be placed. If there are frequent daily services, the vestments may properly be laid out in a drawer of the vestment chest if preferred. Eucharistic vestments are laid out in the following order:

1. Chasuble, front down.
2. Maniple, when used, laid in the center on the orphrey of the chasuble. This forms the "I" of the sacred monogram "IHS."
3. Stole, laid with the neckband across the maniple and the ends raised on each side to form the "H."
4. White rope girdle, folded evenly together and curled around to form the "S" of the monogram.

5. Alb, front down, unbuttoned, with the skirt folded up and then back so that the hem will be at the edge of the table.
6. Amice, if used, front down with strings crossed.

A linen cloth, matching the bottom cloth, should be laid over the vestments if they are not to be worn immediately. It should have a plain colored cross upon it, preferably blue, about three inches square. This cloth is removed by the Altar Guild worker before the priest arrives to vest for the service.

After the service is over and the congregation dispersed, the vessels and linens are removed from the altar to the sacristy. The chalice and paten should be rinsed with cold water and the water poured into a piscina or the ground. The vessels should then be thoroughly scalded, wiped dry with a soft cloth used for no other purpose, and put away in their cases. The used linens should be rinsed, wrapped together and taken home to be carefully laundered. The eucharistic candles are removed from the altar (unless they are the only candles) and the altar book and its stand put in the sacristy or placed on the credence. The altar is then covered with the dust protector, carefully spread.

The Symbol—The IHS, the Sacred Monogram, is made up of the first three letters of the Greek word for Jesus.

If for any reason the flowers are to be left until the next day they should have fresh water. Flowers should not be left upon an altar after they start to wither, and empty vases should be removed, not left as ornaments.

The alms should be put in a bank bag or suitable container for the church treasurer to pick up.

Used vestments should be put away to be pressed or laundered and both sanctuary and sacristy left in perfect order.

In churches with traditional altars against the wall there will be little change as far as the Altar Guild is concerned. The priest will decide how best to make any adjustments. For churches with the altar standing free so that the celebrant may face the people from behind it, here is a suggested form of procedure.

The priest may begin the Holy Communion at a prayer desk or a side table or in choir instead of at the altar. If so, the chalice may be put on the credence with the elements. Some churches have the elements brought by laypersons from the back of the church to the sanctuary along with the alms basins. The eucharistic candles are put on the altar and the altar book on its stand on the epistle side. If eucharistic vestments are worn, the chasuble may be laid on the end of the altar, or over the communion rail. In that case, the rest of the eucharistic vesture is laid out in the sacristy in this order: stole, girdle, alb and amice. The celebrant will wear these into the sanctuary, and after the Ministry of the Word will put on the chasuble. The chalice will be brought to the altar from the credence. Other arrangements may be worked out by the priest or as directed by the bishop.

HOLY BAPTISM

Baptism takes place at the font, which is usually near the door of the church. The font must be cleaned and dusted before a baptism is to take place.

As Holy Baptism is a corporate service in which the whole Body of Christ participates and the congregation act as witnesses, it is much preferred that baptism take place at regular church services. Each candidate is to be sponsored by one or more baptized persons.

When there is a baptistry altar with cross and candlesticks, and the baptism takes place at a regular church service, the acolyte may light the candles at the time of the baptism. At a private service prepared for by the Altar Guild, the member on duty should light the candles before the family assembles, if no acolyte is to be present.

Vessels and linen necessary for a baptism:

1. Ewer, containing warm water
2. Baptismal bowl, if used
3. Baptismal shell
4. Baptismal towel
5. Pascal Candle, if used
6. Baptismal Candle, if used
7. The certificate near at hand
8. Prayer Book for priest, marked at Holy Baptism
9. Prayer Books for parents, sponsors and witnesses, also properly marked; or the Holy Baptism booklets, if used.

The ewer may be placed on the baptistry altar, or on a suitable table, or on steps by the font.

Often the font has an outlet with stopper and the water is poured by the officiant into the font itself. Generally the stop-

---

The Symbol—Symbol for the Church, the Body of Christ, the redemptive society. The ship, with the cross as mast, carries the faithful over the sea of life to eternity. The fish, ICTHUS, is the early Christian symbol for "Jesus Christ, Son of God, Saviour." May be used as a symbol for Baptism. One becomes a member of the Church and is cleansed of sins through washing with water.

per is removed at the end of the service just before leaving the font.

When a baptismal bowl is used, it is put in the font with the shell either in it or beside it, and the towel is laid on the altar or over the edge of the font, whichever seems more convenient.

If the font has no outlet, after the service the water should be carefully taken up and poured upon the ground and the font thoroughly dried. The interior bowl of the font should be kept clean at all times. The font should never be used to hold floral decorations

White is the normal liturgical color for the baptismal rite of initiation.

"Holy Baptism is especially appropriate at the Easter Vigil, on the Day of Pentecost, on All Saints' Day or the Sunday after All Saints' Day, and on the Feast of the Baptism of our Lord (the First Sunday after the Epiphany). It is recommended that, as far as possible, Baptisms be reserved for these occasions or when a bishop is present."

—The Book of Common Prayer

THE ORDER OF CONFIRMATION

The altar setting for the Order of Confirmation depends upon the type of service at which the Confirmation is to take place, that is, whether the service is Holy Communion or Morning or Evening Prayer. Frequently, however, it is a special service and if so, the altar should be covered with the prayer cloth over its standard vestments.

The color for confirmation is red (though white is often used), and if red flowers of a suitable kind are obtainable, these would be most appropriate. White flowers may also be used or a carefully chosen combination of the two colors.

Since confirmation may rightly be thought of as an ordination of the laity, a special candle signifying the presence of the bishop of the diocese may be put upon the retable or altar, gospel side, next to the cross. In some dioceses this is done only at ordinations. If the officiating bishop at confirmation is other than the diocesan, the candle is omitted.

The bishop usually brings his own vestments and equipment. The vestments worn by the attending clergy are those of local custom with the stoles usually red. Each bishop has his own method of procedure and, if necessary, will give instructions to the rector to pass on to the Altar Guild workers.

FIRST COMMUNION

The admission of young children to the Holy Communion will sometimes take place on a special occasion developed within an individual parish's tradition. An early Christmas Eve service has been used in some churches with success.

The Altar Guild responsibilities on this occasion will be the same as for any eucharist. Special directions may be given by the rector for this particular service.

Some parishes are now using the "confirmation veil" as a First Communion veil. These are of white voile or organdy, easily made, cut about thirty to thirty-six inches square with one and one-half inch hem. A yard of white silk ribbon or tape may be stitched for about ten inches at the underside of the top center, to go around the head and tie under the hair in back. It is best to have two sizes of veils. The veils should always be kept clean and be pressed before each use.

Altar Guild members are responsible for putting the veils on the young ladies and for collecting them after the service. Pins should be provided, if needed, to hold the veils at the top of the hair.

All should be veiled and in readiness a half hour before the service to avoid last minute confusion, and the work should be done well out of the way of the vesting clergy.

The Symbol—The Bishop's mitre: symbol of the Episcopacy. Used symbolically to designate any rites or ceremonies at which Episcopal ministrations are required, such as confirmations, ordinations, consecrations, dedications.

2

Festivals and Seasons

* * * * *

ADVENT

The shell symbolizes *Baptism*, which is our entrance to the Christian, and Church's life. The Church year begins with *Advent*, the penitential season which precedes Christmas.

There are four Sundays in Advent, and the color used is purple. As will be mentioned later in Chapter 7, under "Flowers," some churches do not use flowers on the altar during Advent because of the nature of this season of prayer and

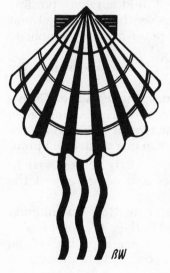

The Symbol—Advent: from the liturgical Gospels for Advent. St. John Baptist, Third Sunday: St. Matthew 21, "Behold I send my messenger . . . which shall prepare thy way before thee." Fourth Sunday: John 1:26, "John answered . . . I baptize with water." The shell is the traditional symbol for Holy Baptism.

preparation for the coming of Christ. The word "advent" means "coming." If flowers *are* used they should not be the white of festivals but should harmonize with the violet vestments and hangings.

THE NATIVITY OF OUR LORD JESUS CHRIST, OR CHRISTMAS
The altar must be the center of attention and no decorating done which detracts from it. It should be thoroughly cleaned and fresh linens used throughout, the best the church affords. New candles should be put in all candlesticks and the candlesticks polished.

White flowers should be used in the vases or containers. Plants of red poinsettia, so lovely at Christmas, make the most effective setting when suitably and artistically arranged. These may be used to supplement the vases. All should be grouped with the cross as the focal point. The pots of any plants used should be wrapped in white crepe paper, not the glittering silver or red favored by florists. If the sanctuary is large enough to permit the placing of Christmas trees at the back corners, these may be used undecorated, possibly banked with greens at the foot to cover the stands. Restraint must be evident in the result, never over-dressing. Simplicity is the greatest beauty.

As mentioned under Baptism, floral decorations must not be put in the font.

In many Episcopal churches today, the festival of Christmas begins with a choral celebration of the Holy Communion at midnight on Christmas Eve. The altar is prepared for the Holy Communion and since more than one chalice will probably be needed, these should be properly placed well in advance of the time of the service and before any of the congregation is present.

As explained under preparation for the Holy Communion in Chapter 1, the corporal is spread in the center at the edge of the fair linen and the vested chalice placed just back of the corporal cross. The fair linen must come only to the edge of the atlar; *in no case* must it hang over. If it is necessary to use a fair linen which may be too large, it can be folded under at the back.

Extra candelabra may be placed upon the altar, arranged so as not to interfere with the celebrant's preparation of the chalices, and symmetrically distant from the back and the sides of the altar. The two eucharistic candlesticks should also be used.

The altar service book on its stand sits on the epistle side of the altar facing the celebrant, closed. A white marker is used for it, properly placed at the collect for Christmas and at the beginning of the communion service.

On the credence table are placed the wine and water cruets and supplementary flagons if needed, the bread box with extra bread, the lavabo bowl and lavabo towel. If so directed, the elements may be brought from a side altar or the back or elsewhere in the church and brought to the altar along with the alms basins.

Alms basins are put in readiness.

The first service on Christmas Day is usually an early celebration of the Holy Communion without music. The altar is prepared for this with only the two traditional eucharistic candles, the chalice or chalices as above, and the missal on its stand.

If one or more later choral eucharists are scheduled, extra candelabra may be added to the altar to augment the two eucharistic candles. These extra candles should not be added or used unless they are to be lighted. They should not be used

---

The Symbol—Christmas: The manger-bed with the Christ Child. The nimbus (often called the halo) surrounding the head denotes sanctity. The star form is actually an *Iota Chi*, the initials in Greek of Jesus Christ.

just for show. At celebrations without music they should be omitted.

An exception to the use of unlighted candles is that when the six office lights are a permanent part of the altar setting, they may remain unlighted at early celebrations of the Holy Communion.

White is the liturgical color for this season.

In procession at the choral eucharist on festivals, the celebrant may wear a cope, which adds beauty and dignity to the service. Under this is worn the eucharistic vestments, without the chasuble. Upon reaching the sanctuary in procession, the celebrant may go into the sacristy while the choir is finishing the hymn or introit and remove the cope. If more convenient the change may be made at the sedilia or kneeling at the side on the altar step and assisted by other members of the clergy, lay ministers or acolytes. The procedure which is most inconspicuous is the one which should be used.

When the celebrant is the only minister present and eucharistic vestments are used in procession only the alb, amice, girdle and stole are worn. The chasuble is then put on at the offertory.

At the conclusion of the last service of Christmas it is a nice custom to have the plants and flowers from the altar taken to the parish sick, with an appropriate card. Flowers must not be left upon the altar to wither.

The greens and decorations should stay up through the Epiphany on January sixth. They must be taken down at the close of the Epiphany octave, at the latest.

THE EPIPHANY

The Gospel for the Epiphany is the lovely story of the coming of the Wise Men. It comes twelve days after Christmas, on January sixth. The color is white.

On the first Sunday following the Epiphany, many churches have a late afternoon or evening candlelight service, often with a children's pageant portraying the coming of the Wise Men to the manger. Candlelight services vary, but candle supply

companies have candlelight service sets which may be adapted to the particular need. If there is a pageant, the procedure can be so ordered as to fit the size and ability of the group. One altar setting will be given here.

A CANDLELIGHT SERVICE

It is best to cover the altar with a white cloth over the prayer cloth to protect it from wax. A large candlestick with a candle representing Christ is placed in the center of the altar, slightly back. Before it are twelve smaller candles representing the twelve apostles. A narrow, wooden board about the length of the altar, with holes made in it in which to put the candles, will have to be provided. Cardboard will do it if it is stiff enough to hold the candles upright. The twelve candles should be evenly spaced. In front of the board, one near each end, place two candlesticks containing candles of the same size or similar to those in the board. These represent the apostolic succession of bishops and the diocesan bishop. When arranged, the result should be this:

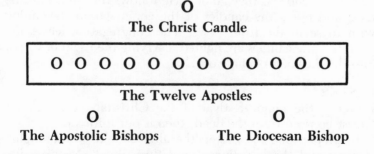

O

The Christ Candle

O O O O O O O O O O O O

The Twelve Apostles

O   O

The Apostolic Bishops   The Diocesan Bishop

The Symbol—Epiphany: the symbols suggest (1) three magi, three crowns; (2) the manifestation of Christ to the world as light falls from the Epiphany Star, spreading in a cross-form, wide to the ends of the earth.

Small candles in paper holders, which come in the candle-light service set, are distributed to the congregation at the door upon entering the church. These are also given to the children of the junior choir, either before the service or as they go by the door in the processional hymn.

White flowers should be provided for the altar, perhaps left from the morning service.

The service begins with a hymn, followed by the opening sentences and prayers. An explanation of the service is then given by the priest. The Old Testament prophecy is read from Isaiah 9:6, and the coming of Christ is told from St. Luke 2:1–16. During this reading, the characters in the pageant arrange themselves.

The choir then sings a Christmas hymn while an acolyte lights the Christ candle and the apostle candles.

The story is then read of the coming of the Wise Men, from St. Matthew 2:1–12, and the calling of the apostles, from St. Matthew 10:2–4. The acolyte stands by and extinguishes the last apostle candle to denote Judas' betrayal of Jesus.

Acts 1:15–26 is now read, and the candle re-lit as Matthias is called to replace Judas. The choir sings as the two bishop candles are lighted. Here the pageant acts out its story.

The benediction and recessional follow. At the beginning of the recessional hymn, the acolyte lights his taper from the diocesan bishop candle and proceeds to light the small can-dles of the choir as they go out. He follows the choir into the nave and lights the candles of the congregation, beginning with those in the front pews. The congregation leaves the church as the candles are lighted, carrying the Light of Christ into the darkness of the world.

EASTER
Easter is the major festival of the Christian year. "Unless Christ be risen from the dead, then is our faith vain."

In preparation for Easter, the altar should be thoroughly cleaned and the best linens used throughout. New candles should be used in the candlesticks and the sticks polished.

Only the two eucharistic candles should be used at an early celebration of the Holy Communion if there is no music. Extra candelabra may be added for choral celebrations later. These should not be put upon the altar unless they are to be lighted.

The paschal candle is lighted during all services and should be attended to immediately upon the arrival of the Altar Guild worker, or possibly the verger, and before any of the congregation is present.

If only one chalice is needed, it may be carried to the altar by the celebrant or placed in position well in advance of the arrival of the congregation. When several chalices are required, they should be placed as directed under the instructions for Christmas, with the veiled chalice on the spread corporal in front and the extra chalices, covered with patens or palls, on the credence. These are brought to the celebrant by the server at the proper time.

Extra purificators may be placed to the right on the fair linen, or left in the burse.

The missal, correctly marked with a white ribbon, goes on its stand on the epistle side of the altar.

On the credence go the filled cruets, with handles to the back to facilitate handing from the server to the celebrant. Also on the credence go the bread box, lavabo bowl and towel, and flagons.

Alms basins should be in readiness, either on or under a credence table, or on a shelf or in their own niche.

White lilies are ever associated with the Resurrection and these flowers are the perfect complement to the Easter setting. If pots of lilies are used as well as cut flowers, the pots should be wrapped in white crepe paper. No decorations should be put where they will hamper the clergy as they go about their ministrations in the sanctuary. Care and artistry must be used in the arrangements of any floral tributes and again, simplicity is best.

White vestments are worn by the clergy. Eucharistic vestments may be worn by the celebrant, or surplices and white stoles by all officiating clergy. In procession the celebrant may wear a festival cope, and upon reaching the sanctuary he may change the cope for the chasuble. All eucharistic vestments except the chasuble and maniple are worn under the cope. The chasuble is not worn in procession nor into the pulpit.

After the last service of Easter Day, the pots of lilies should be taken from the altar and either sent to the parish sick or distributed according to the parish custom. Some churches have a children's service on Easter afternoon when small pots of flowers as symbols of the Resurrection are distributed to the church school children.

If there is a daily service in the church during the Easter octave, the cut lilies may be left in the vases as long as they are fresh. Fading flowers or empty containers must not be left on an altar.

When the day's work is over, the dust protector is put upon the altar, and the sanctuary and sacristy left clean and in order. All used linens should be taken home and carefully laundered.

The Symbol—Easter: the empty cross stands victorious upon three steps representing faith, hope, and charity, surrounded by the circle representing eternity. The lily represents resurrection, for from a seemingly dead bulb springs this new, glorious creation.

ASCENSION DAY

The color is white. This day comes forty days after Easter. The paschal candle, which, if used, has been burning for all services since Easter Day, is finally put out after the reading of the Gospel on this day. An extinguisher should be placed near the altar for the convenience of the celebrant or server. After the service, the paschal candlestick should be carefully cleaned, wrapped in cloth, and stored. Whatever portion of the candle remains may be used as a baptismal candle or wrapped in paper and stored for use in another year at a side or chapel altar.

PENTECOST

The Day of Pentecost, formerly known as Whitsunday, comes the fifieth day after Easter and commemorates the descent of the Holy Spirit upon the apostles. It is one of the major holy days of the Church year and deserves special attention. Red is the color for this principal feast.

If red gladioli are obtainable, they are most appropriate for the altar flowers. They give the appearance of spears like "tongues of fire," very symbolic for this day.

The Symbol—Ascensiontide: The *Chi Rho*, the two letters of the Greek word for Christ. The crown symbolizes that Christ reigns in victory—kingship; the auriole symbolizes glory.

Note: The descending dove with the cruciform nimbus is the symbol of The Holy Spirit.

Red vestments are worn by the clergy, either red eucharistic vestments for a celebration of the Holy Communion, or red stoles. As Pentecost is a major festival, the cope may be worn in procession at a choral celebration of the Holy Communion.

PENTECOST/TRINITY

The season after Pentecost is the longest in the Church year, roughly six months. Trinity Sunday is always the next after Pentecost. The color for Trinity Sunday is white and for the season, green.

OTHER FESTIVALS

THE HOLY NAME, January 1st. The color is white. This is the day our Lord received His Holy Name. Formerly known as The Circumcision of Christ.

THE CONVERSION OF ST. PAUL, January 25th. The color is white.

THE PRESENTATION, February 2nd. The color is white. This day is also called The Purification of St. Mary the Virgin, and "Candlemas." If there is a celebration of the Holy Communion in the church on this day, new eucharistic candles should be used. Any other candles used should also be new. Sometimes a blessing of candles takes place.

THE ANNUNCIATION OF THE BLESSED VIRGIN MARY, March 25th. The color is white. This feast has one of the loveliest collects in the Prayer Book.

ST. MARK THE EVANGELIST, April 25th. The color is red.

THE VISITATION, May 31st. The color is white.

ST. JOHN BAPTIST, June 24th. The color is white because this day commemorates his nativity, not his martyrdom.

The Symbol: Three entwined circles symbolize the eternal quality of the Holy Trinity.

INDEPENDENCE DAY, July 4th. The color is white.

THE TRANSFIGURATION OF CHRIST, August 6th. The color is white.

ST. MARY THE VIRGIN, August 15th. The color is white.

HOLY CROSS DAY, September 14th. The color is white.

ST. MICHAEL AND ALL ANGELS, September 29th. The color is white.

ST. LUKE THE EVANGELIST, October 18th. The color is red.

ALL SAINTS' DAY, November 1st. The color is white.

NATIONAL THANKSGIVING DAY. The color is white. There is usually a service in the church on this day. Instead of putting flowers on the altar, it is an appealing and symbolic custom to offer the fruits of the harvest. Apples, oranges, grapes, gourds, acorn squash—a combination of these, tastefully arranged with greens, makes a most attractive setting. Sheaves of wheat and ears of colored corn, with their shocks, may be used in place of some of the fruit. Wicker cornucopias placed one on each side, open toward the cross and filled to overflowing, will add to the effect.

ST. STEPHEN, December 26th. The color is red. St. Stephen was the first martyr.

ST. JOHN, APOSTLE AND EVANGELIST, December 27th. The color is white.

THE HOLY INNOCENTS, December 28th. The color is purple, unless the day falls on Sunday, when it is red.

THE NAME DAYS OF THE TWELVE APOSTLES:

St. Andrew, November 30th. The color is red.

St. Thomas, December 21st. The color is red.

St. Matthias, February 24th. The color is red.

St. Philip and St. James, May 1st. The color is red.

St. Barnabas, June 11th. The color is red.

St. Peter, June 29th. The color is red.

St. James, July 25th. The color is red.

St. Bartholomew, August 24th. The color is red.

St. Matthew, September 21st. The color is red.

St. Simon and St. Jude, October 28th. The color is red.

The above are all Holy Days of obligation and should not be forgotten by the Christian faithful.

Parishes which have a daily celebration of the Holy Communion provide a rich source of learning for Altar Guilds, and members should be familiar with *Lesser Feasts and Fasts*, the short name for the expanded Calendar and compilation of a series of collects, psalms, and lessons for the Minor Holy Days, authorized by the General Convention of our Church. Such calendars as *The New Episcopal Church Calendar*, and others, indicate when these days occur and give proper colors, along with Bible lessons for Morning and Evening Prayer for each day.

The Symbol—"He shall rule unto the ends of the earth." The symbol suggests (1) Missions: the Gospel carried to the ends of the earth; (2) the saints who have carried the Good News and established a redemptive society in all places on the globe—they who have preached the Gospel through word and deed.

3

Lent

Ash Wednesday through Saturday, Easter Even

* * * * *

Lent is the penitential season of forty days preceding Easter and begins with Ash Wednesday. No flowers should be used on the altar during Lent. Some churches make an exception of the 4th Sunday in Lent, sometimes called "Laetare" Sunday. However, Lent is a disciplinary period and cannot well fulfill its intent and meaning if exceptions are made.

ASH WEDNESDAY
"Remember, O man, that dust thou art and unto dust thou shalt return."

The Book of Common Prayer provides a special liturgy for Ash Wednesday. It includes the Litany of Penitence. Most churches observe this first day of Lent with celebration of the Holy Communion, with varying degrees of ceremonial.

Some churches follow the custom, which came into general use in the Middle Ages, of the imposition of ashes. If so, the women of the Altar Guild must know what preparation to make for this.

On Shrove Tuesday, the day before Ash Wednesday, materials should be assembled in the sacristy. The ashes are obtained by burning the palm blessed on the previous Palm Sunday and kept for this purpose. If none has been reserved at the church, the members of the Altar Guild could bring

from home the palm fronds or crosses they have kept. A small pan should be provided in which to burn the palm. The ashes are put in a small metal or glass bowl, covered with a linen towel and left in the sacristy overnight. Before the first service of Holy Communion on Ash Wednesday, the bowl is put on the credence table along with the appointments necessary for the service. If the priest prefers, it may be put on the altar.

Any ashes remaining should be either washed down the piscina or spread on the ground.

If the Great Litany is said, a prayer desk should be put on the nave floor at the center or side of the chancel steps, so that the minister may kneel facing the altar.

SUNDAY OF THE PASSION, OR PALM SUNDAY

On Saturday, the day before Passion or Palm Sunday, the crosses and crucifixes in the church and chapel, and also in the sacristies and offices, should be veiled in violet or purple.

Paintings and pictures in the church may be otherwise veiled, but not the Stations of the Cross. The material used is silk crepe, or its equivalent, and the draping must be done with care and restraint. The purple veiling stays on (with exceptions which will be noted) until Easter Eve.

The altar veils cover the cross completely and may be either gathered under the foot or left

The Symbol—Lent: The *Agnus Dei*, meaning the Lamb of God, represents Christ's sacrifice.

The Symbol—Passiontide: the cross with the crown of thorns and nails represents the Passion of our Lord.

hanging loose if they are not too long. They may be confined above the base of the cross with a very narrow silk cord, or thread, of matching color.

Processional crosses for church and church school are also veiled, the veiling being tied with narrow ribbon to match, with the ends of the veiling hanging free.

Palm ordered from commercial supply houses usually comes in bunches or "heads" wrapped in burlap. These should be promptly immersed, burlap and all, in a deep container of water. They may be kept thus, in a cool place, for a week or more.

On the day before Palm Sunday, a group of Altar Guild women, or a youth group of the parish under adult supervision, should assemble to make crosses of palm for the congregation and church school.

Crosses may be made in various designs. When a large number is needed, simple ones with the cross strip slipped through a slit in the shaft are most quickly made. Two designs for more appealing ones will be given on the following pages. These take considerable time to make but are worth the effort. The crosses should be kept overnight between damp terry cloth towels. They must not dry out. Plain strips of palm, single or double, may also be used.

In ample time before the first service of Palm Sunday, the crosses and palm strips should be put in a plain woven basket, or other suitable container, and put on the end of the altar for blessing. If strips are used, they should be tied in a bundle. After the blessing, which usually comes at the beginning of the service, an acolyte or usher takes them to the rear of the church for distribution to the people when the service is concluded. Methods of distribution vary in different churches.

When making the crosses, palm fronds can be set aside for the choir to carry in procession. These also must be wrapped in damp towels overnight.

When large pieces of palm are desired for decoration, they may be tacked on strips of light wood to hold them in place.

Palm fronds in a fan-like arrangement may be put in the altar vases.

Palm fronds may be slipped through the ribbon tying the veil of the processional cross.

A few crosses or strips of palm should be reserved for the imposition of ashes on the next Ash Wednesday if it is the custom. Any others remaining after the services should be burned. All palm, wherever put, must be removed and burned at the close of the day.

Palm crosses and fronds that are taken home should be carefully kept from Palm Sunday until the next Ash Wednesday, when they should be reverently burned.

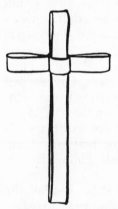

Pattern No. 1 for Palm Crosses

A palm frond about ¼ inch wide and 13 inches long will make an average size cross.

(1) Hold the frond horizontally.

(2) Bend the right end straight up from the center to form a right angle.

(3) Fold this same top strip, from the center, back and down, up and over again, to form a square at the back. It will still be a right angle.

(4) Bring the left strip forward and fold over the center toward the right. Fold away from you and pull through the square at back, all the way.

(5) Bend the top strip forward and put the end through the center square to make a shaft of desired length.

(6) Fold left hand strip backwards and put through the back square. This makes the left cross-bar and should be in proportion to the shaft.

(7) Fold the right strip back, put through the back square and fasten.

Pattern No. 2 for Palm Crosses

Take a palm frond about ¹/₂ inch wide and hold upright.
(1) Fold the top down, away from you, and the bottom up, away from you, to form the shaft of a cross of desired length.
(2) Turn the end down and twist around to the right and across the front of the shaft to make a cross-bar in proportion to the length.
(3) Fold the end around behind the shaft.
(4) Bring the end from behind, under the center. Fold from the bottom right to the top left and under again from the bottom left to the top right.
(5) Fasten the end through the back loops to lock.

HOLY WEEK

Most churches have a daily celebration of the eucharist during Holy Week, this most solemn week of the Church year. On Monday, Tuesday, and Wednesday, the celebration is usually the same as on other days.

A CHALICE   **A PATEN**   **A CIBORIUM**

MAUNDY THURSDAY has special significance, since it commemorates the institution of the Lord's Supper. For this observance, the altar is in festival dress. The cross is veiled in white, altar flowers are white, as are the celebrant's vestments. The chalice is also vested in white.

Some churches will include the ancient ceremony of the washing of the feet at the last celebration on Maundy Thursday. This ceremony, according to the Prayer Book, appropriately follows the Gospel and homily.

After the last celebration on Maundy Thursday, many churches keep a Vigil or Watch before the reserved Blessed Sacrament. If the church has a chapel or side altar, the vigil is prepared for there as follows: the sacrament, covered with a white lace veil, is placed in the tabernacle with the door left open. If there is no tabernacle the sacrament is placed upon the altar, veiled as stated, with a vigil light burning before it.

Traditionally the vigil lasts until Good Friday morning. However, in some parishes the watch is kept only until night on Thursday. Where the longer watch is kept, the sacrament is carried back to the main altar at the proper time in the service on Good Friday (at the Mass of the Pre-Sanctified). Where the Mass of the Pre-Sanctified is not observed on Good Friday, the rector will probably arrange some suitable place to which the reserved sacrament may be removed after the close of the vigil. The sacrament should not be publicly reserved in the church on Good Friday other than in relation to the Mass of the Pre-Sanctified. These are matters in which the rector should give direction.

When there is the Mass on Good Friday, the Sacrament for Maundy Thursday before which the vigil was kept is the Pre-Sanctified Host for the Mass. This must be especially prepared for by placing two priests' hosts on the paten when vesting the chalice for the celebration of Maundy Thursday.

At this time, also, a ciborium, or an extra chalice and paten, covered with a white lace veil are put upon the altar to receive the second consecrated host. At the conclusion of the Maundy Thursday service, this ciborium, or the chalice and paten, veiled, is the one which is exposed for the vigil. Either a sanctuary lamp or a votive light should burn before it. Some churches use a red light, some prefer white.

If there is no tabernacle in which to reserve the Host, some suitable aumbry must be provided in the sacristy to house It over Maundy Thursday night. It may from there be brought to the altar by the priest on Good Friday morning.

At the close of the Maundy Thursday observances, the white altar is dismantled, the cross veiled in black, and the altar stripped for Good Friday. Any other crosses or crucifixes in the church should also be veiled in black. The crosses in the sacristies and offices remain veiled in purple, as they have been since Passion Sunday. For the observance of Maundy Thursday, only the cross of the altar upon which the Holy Communion is celebrated, and the vigil altar if it is not the same one, are veiled in white, no others.

The procedure when Maundy Thursday ends will depend somewhat on whether the sacrament is reserved at the main altar, or at a chapel or side altar, or not at all.

For Good Friday the candles should be removed from the altar and retables and the altar left bare. Covers should be removed from the credence tables and the sanctuary cleared of any removable ornaments.

GOOD FRIDAY
The Book of Common Prayer contains a special liturgy for Good Friday.

This is a very dramatic service, symbolizing the utter confusion of the apostles at the death of the Lord

For the THREE HOUR SERVICE, the sanctuary remains the same. The clergy are vested in cassocks, no surplices. If there is a choir, they also wear cassocks, no cottas. The same applies to the acolytes.

If there is an evening service, perhaps with a sacred cantata, the clergy and acolytes wear black cassocks, no surplices or cottas. No processional cross precedes their entrance.

THE CRUCIFIX: A SYMBOL OF THE CRUCIFIXION

HOLY SATURDAY AND THE GREAT VIGIL OF EASTER

When there is a service on Holy Saturday, it should conform to the instructions in the Prayer Book. The special rite for the Liturgy of the Word may be used as may be Morning Prayer. There is no celebration of the eucharist on this day and the people do not communicate.

After noon on Holy Saturday, preparation may be begun for Easter Day. The paschal candle should be made ready. It has its special candlestick which should be placed on the sanctuary floor, gospel side. The priest usually inserts the incense nails at the service of its lighting. If however the clergy prefer this be done by the Altar Guild earlier in the day, the procedure is as follows. The nails, representing the Five Wounds of our Lord, are inserted in designated grooves in the candle from the top down and left to right, forming a cross thus:

1

4 2 5

3

It is helpful in inserting them if each nail is touched quickly to a lighted candle stub first. This seals them tightly without danger of breaking.

The paschal candle symbolizes the forty days our Lord was on earth after His Resurrection. Since it signifies His being alive, the congregation should not see the candle unlighted. Except for the Easter Vigil service, the Altar Guild worker coming to prepare for a service should light it immediately upon arrival, before the congregation assembles, and it must remain lighted until all have departed. Acolytes should be instructed not to extinguish it along with the altar candles. It cannot, unfortunately, be left burning throughout the night because of the fire hazard, but its significance for the congregation may nevertheless be preserved. It is finally extinguished by the priest, or acolyte, after the reading of the gospel on the Ascension Day. It is removed from the sanctuary after the close of the last service on that day. The paschal candle is normally used at baptisms throughout the year.

The liturgy for the Great Vigil of Easter may require substantial preparation as it is not only the first eucharist of Easter but it is also a time at which we recall the great events of our salvation history. It may be a time of baptisms and confirmations. The liturgy is most dramatic and many churches are tending to use this service as an Easter "Midnight Mass."

4

Weddings

* * * * *

Regulations governing weddings and proper reverence and respect for the church must be tactfully explained to people planning to use its facilities. This particularly applies to those who seldom feel the need of the church at other times and are not familiar with the procedure at weddings nor with the general customs of church behavior.

Altar Guild members are in charge of wedding arrangements for the church, carrying out the rector's instructions, and no professional wedding arrangers or friends of the participating parties with plans and ideas foreign to the Church's traditions should supersede them. Nor should these people be present at the rehearsal, which is handled by the rector and is attended only by members of the bridal party.

White is the traditional color for weddings. A white frontal, clean altar linens, and new candles should be used. The fair linen is covered with the prayer cloth.

White flowers are arranged in the vases. No florists or professional decorators should be permitted to place the altar flowers, and no decorations other than these should be put in the sanctuary. If more elaborate flower arrangements are desired, they may be carried out in the church proper. Baskets of flowers on stands might be put at the chancel steps and garlands on the pews, provided they are in good taste and not overdone. The altar flowers should remain at the church, but the flower baskets could be used for the reception afterwards if desired. The simpler the decorating, the more the church will look as it should, with quiet beauty.

Branch candelabra may be put upon the altar to add to the festive look, and extra floor candelabra may be put in the choir pews. These latter must be carefully placed so that they will not interfere with the procession and so that the whole will give a balanced and harmonious effect.

A white canvas runner may be laid in the aisle, covering the step upon which the wedding pillow rests and extending the length of the aisle. If a single length only is desired, it may be folded at the foot of the chancel steps with the end on top so that it may be pulled to the rear by the ushers when the procession is to begin. If a double length is used, the wedding guests walk upon the bottom half and the top is folded at the foot of the chancel steps to be pulled to the rear. The runner is usually brought by the florist along with the wedding flowers, and Altar Guild members should supervise the laying of the runner to see that it is correctly done.

A wedding pillow of white silk or satin should be provided by the Altar Guild for all weddings. In small churches with few weddings or limited funds, any suitable pillow might be covered with a white silk slipcover.

All of these arrangements should be completed well in advance of the arrival of the wedding guests, and the Altar Guild will then be free to assist the priest or bridal party.

The priest will be vested as custom in white stole. Some priests also wear a cope at weddings.

Most churches have fixed fees for weddings, and questions regarding them should be referred to the rector. If asked privately concerning a fee for the rector himself, suggest that a sum be given in accordance with the financial ability of the family.

WEDDING PROCEDURE

Priests differ somewhat in their ideas of wedding procedure, but most arrangements are substantially the same. A standard procedure is as follows:

Candles should be lighted and the music should begin about twenty minutes before the ceremony. The wedding ceremony should begin on time.

A moment or two before, two ushers are told to escort the mothers into the church. The bridal party waits in the rear of the church until the mothers are seated.

The groom's mother goes first, holding the usher's right arm. She sits in the front pew on the right side of the aisle. Any other members of the groom's family, including his father (unless he attends the groom as best man), should already be seated there.

The bride's mother follows, on the usher's left arm. She sits in the front pew on the left. Her family also should be previously seated. The same usher may seat both mothers, if necessary, returning to the rear for the bride's mother after seating the groom's.

When a runner is used, if different ushers seat the two mothers, the first usher waits at the front pew for the arrival of the second in order that both may then pull the runner to the rear for the bridal procession. The runner must be pulled smooth and fall evenly.

Immediately upon their return, the signal is given the organist for the wedding march to begin. A member of the

The Symbol—Marriage: the *Chi Rho* symbolizes Christ who binds and blesses the bridal couple; the two rings symbolize the two persons joined in Holy Matrimony; and the six stone waterpots remind us that Christ turned water into wine at the first miracle performed at the marriage feast in Cana, thus sanctifying marriage.

Altar Guild may wait conveniently to give the signal.

Instead of the usual march, a growing custom in the Episcopal Church is to sing a hymn as the bridal procession comes to the sanctuary and another as it goes out.

As soon as the wedding music begins, the ushers start down the aisle either singly, or two by two if there are a number of them. The same Altar Guild member who signaled the organist may now see that the procession moves forward properly.

As soon as the ushers start, the groom and best man come in from a side entrance and take their places, on the right, at the foot of the chancel steps. The priest comes in from the sacristy with his attendant, if any, and stands at the top of the chancel steps.

The ushers are followed by the bridesmaids, walking alone. If there are a number of bridesmaids, as many as eight or ten, they walk in pairs, the width of the church aisle permitting.

The maid, or matron, of honor follows the last bridesmaid, just preceding the bride.

If there is a flower girl, or a small boy bearing the ring, she or he should just precede the maid of honor. If there are both flower girl and ring bearer, they walk together preceding the maid of honor.

The bride comes last, with her father, or whoever gives her away. She holds his left arm.

Upon reaching the chancel steps, the ushers line up to the right of the groom and best man. The bridesmaids go to the left side of the chancel steps.

After the betrothals are read, the priest turns and goes up to the altar. The bridal couple follows and stands at the rail, facing the altar. When they are in place, the bridesmaids and ushers follow, preceded by the maid of honor and the best man. The flower girl and ring bearer, if any, follow the maid of honor and best man, ahead of the bridesmaids. The first bridesmaid takes the arm of the first usher, and so on, two by two. They separate just behind the bride and groom and go to the right and left as they were before, now lining the communion rail.

Where space or design of the chancel present a problem, only the four principals go to the altar rail, after the betrothals are read, and the rest of the bridal party remain at the foot of the chancel steps.

The ceremony proceeds, the bride and groom turning towards each other to make their vows, and then kneeling when told.

Upon the completion of the ceremony the music again guides them and the couple march out together. The maid of honor follows with the best man, the flower girl and ring bearer, and the bridesmaids and ushers, two by two.

Immediately after the bridal party has left the church, the ushers return to escort the mothers out. They are followed by the members of their families, after which the wedding guests may leave.

When the pews have been closed in by ribbons, two ushers must return to remove them and let the wedding guests out.

As soon as the bridal party has left the church the candles should be extinguished.

NOTES
The florist should provide both the aisle runner and the pew ribbons, if used.

Photographers are generally not permitted to take pictures in the church while the ceremony is taking place. Pictures may be taken at the church door, on the lawn, or in the parish house. These are matters for the rector to decide. The bride's family could then be informed so that the photographers might be instructed when hired.

THE NUPTIAL EUCHARIST
When the Holy Communion is celebrated at the time a marriage is solemnized, it is called a Nuptial Eucharist or Nuptial Mass.

The altar is prepared beforehand for the Holy Communion, with the two eucharistic candlesticks and the missal on its stand. Fresh linen is used, the chalice vested in white and placed in proper position on the altar. The cruets are filled and, with the bread box, lavabo bowl, and lavabo towel, are put on the credence.

Two priests sometimes officiate at this service, one performing the marriage, the other acting as celebrant at the eucharist. The priest performing the marriage will wear surplice and white stole, and the celebrant will wear white eucharistic vestments, if this is the custom, or both may wear surplices and white stoles. At the conclusion of the marriage ceremony the bride and groom continue to kneel at the communion rail. If the same priest is both officiant and celebrant, the change from surplice to chasuble is made at this point. It may be done either in the sacristy or assisted by the server in the sanctuary—the eucharistic vestments must be in readiness wherever they are donned.

The communion service proceeds as usual from this point. The maid of honor and the best man also kneel at the rail, one at each side, but not too near to the bride and groom. The other bridal attendants go into the pews and kneel there.

At the conclusion of the service, the music heralds the recessional and all go out as described before.

5

Burials

*****

The Burial Service is usually said in the choir, but if necessary in the sanctuary. The altar is vested in the prayer cloth over the fair linen.

Flowers may be put in the vases or containers and colored flowers are to be preferred to white for burials. Varying shades of violet or pastel colors or a suitable combination of the two are most appropriate. White flowers are sometimes requested by the bereaved family, but when the choice is left to the Altar Guild white should be avoided since it is a festival color. It is greatly to be desired that there be no flowers in the church except those on the altar. If it is known that the church has this fixed rule, the parishioners will soon become accustomed to it. A memorial fund could well be set up with the contributions for burial flowers and something of lasting beauty be provided for the church.

Every parish should have a funeral pall, which covers the casket instead of flowers. Thus each casket looks like every other, just as God's love covers all equally, rich and poor alike. No flowers should be put upon the pall. Contributions given instead of flowers might be used to buy the pall, if the parish does not have one.

Funeral palls may be white, black, purple, or green, lined with matching or contrasting color, with or without tassels, and they usually have a cross extending from top to bottom and side to side, across the center. The present trend is to have the white pall symbolizing the hope of the resurrection.

In preparation for burials, the Altar Guild may lay the pall over the last pew at the church door for the undertaker to place upon the casket. After the service he will replace it there for the Altar Guild members to put carefully away.

If flowers are used in the church, cards enclosed with them, if not removed by the undertaker, should be removed by the Altar Guild and given to some representative of the bereaved family.

NOTES

Priests differ in their methods of conducting a burial service. Some have the coffin in place before the chancel steps some time before the service. At the appointed time, the priest comes into the church from the sacristy and begins the service.

Others follow the order of the Book of Common Prayer and, meeting the coffin at the door of the church, go before it in procession down the aisle reading the opening words of the burial service. A crucifer usually precedes the priest, and sometimes torchbearers.

The coffin should be closed during the time it is in the church. It is placed in the nave aisle at the foot of the chancel steps. The coffin of a priest may be put on the chancel pavement if there is room to walk around it.

The family of the deceased usually comes into the church from a side entrance, immediately before the service is to begin, and sits in the front pew or pews.

At the conclusion of the service, the crucifer again leads the procession out of the church, the priest follows, then the pallbearers with the coffin on its carriage, followed by the members of the family. If the members of the family do not wish to do this, they may leave the church by the side entrance through which they entered.

BURIAL OF A CHILD

When the burial is that of a child, a colored pall should not be used. White flowers on the coffin should be used instead, unless there is a white pall available.

Flowers on the altar should be white and the color of the vestments is white.

A REQUIEM
The altar is prepared for the Holy Communion when a requiem is to be said. The chalice is normally vested in white and placed on the altar or credence, depending on the local custom. The eucharistic candles and the missal are put in their usual positions. The missal should have a marker at the burial prayers. The cruets, bread box, lavabo bowl, and lavabo towel are put on the credence table.

BURIALS OUTSIDE THE CHURCH
When a burial service is read at a funeral establishment, a vestment case containing the needed equipment should be packed for the priest. In it should be: a cassock. a cincture, a surplice, a white stole or a tippet, a Prayer Book or a Burial Service Book. A small, lightweight suitcase should be kept in the sacristy for this purpose and for making outside calls of other kinds.

The Prayer Book notes, however, that "Baptized Christians are properly buried from the church. The service should be held at a time when the congregation has opportunity to be present."

6

Special Services

*****

ORDINATIONS

Preparation for ordinations may vary according to the direction of the officiating bishop, but except for details procedure is generally the same.

The altar is set up for the Holy Communion. The vestments may be red or white, depending on the preference of the bishop. The rector can ascertain this when the preliminary arrangements are made. White flowers should be used on the altar if the vestments are white. A suitable combination of red and white flowers such as gladioli, would be better if the vestments are red.

The chalice is vested in the chosen color and put in place on the altar, or if so directed, on the credence.

The attending priests will be vested in stoles of the same color as the chalice vestments.

At 'ordination with Solemn High Mass, the bishop-celebrant is assisted by deacon and sub-deacon, who wear alb, amice, white rope girdle, and maniple; the deacon wears a stole and a dalmatic; the sub-deacon a tunicle.

The ordinand or ordinands will communicate first, then the members of their families, followed by the congregation. The bread box, cruets, lavabo bowl, and lavabo towel go on the credence. Alms basins are put in their usual place.

At all ordinations by the diocesan bishop, a single candle should be put on the retable, gospel side. When there is no retable, it may be put at the back of the altar, gospel side.

Ordination to the Diaconate—Candidates for deacon are vested in a surplice or alb, without tippet or other vesture distinctive of ecclesiastical or academic rank or office.

The dalmatic and the stole are laid over the communion rail, on the epistle side, to be ready for the presenting priest to vest his candidate when the proper time comes in the service.

Each ordinand is presented with a Bible. A small table, covered with a white cloth, should be put on the epistle side of the sanctuary to hold the Bibles.

Ordination to the Priesthood—Candidates for priest are vested in surplice or alb, without stole, tippet or other vesture distinctive of ecclesiastical or academic rank or order.

The chasuble is laid over the communion rail, on the epistle side, to be ready for the presenting priest to vest his candidate.

Each ordinand is presented with a Bible and in some dioceses, a token chalice and paten. A small table covered with a white cloth, on which to put these, should be placed in the sanctuary on the epistle side.

If there is anointing, a linen cloth or small towel should be put on this table for the bishop's use.

CONSECRATION OF A BISHOP

Few churches are fortunate enough to be chosen as the place of consecration of a bishop. Careful preparation must be made by those responsible, and the church will of necessity have to be large enough to accommodate the priests and bishops required to take part in the ceremony.

A bishop is consecrated at a service of Holy Communion, and the altar should be prepared accordingly, with the chalice in place.

The vestment color may be red or white. The flowers are white and should be arranged with very special care. It has been customary to put an extra candle on the gospel side of the altar, to honor the Presiding Bishop-celebrant or his representative.

On the credence table, as usual, go the cruets, bread box, lavabo bowl, and lavabo towel.

The bishop-consecrate is vested in cassock and rochet. The remainder of the episcopal habit is laid over the communion rail, or in a covenient place, so that the attending bishops may vest the new bishop at the proper time in the service.

The new bishop is presented with a Bible.

VISITATION OF A BISHOP

As explained under CONFIRMATION and ORDINATIONS, when the bishop of the diocese visits a church for a service other than the Holy Communion, a single candle is put on the gospel side of the altar or retable. When the visiting bishop is other than the diocesan, this is not done.

A BISHOP IN ROCHET (1) AND CHIMERE (2)

Bishops bring their own episcopal vestments to special services. When celebrating the Holy Communion in a parish where eucharistic vestments are worn, the parish provides these for the bishop.

The visit of the diocesan bishop should be a great occasion in the parish and special care should be taken to have everything in perfect order as far as the Altar Guild is concerned. In his travels about, it is a great joy to one's bishop to see a spotless and correctly appointed altar.

THE DEDICATION AND CONSECRATION OF A CHURCH

The dedication and consecration of a church is done by the diocesan bishop using the form prescribed in the Book of Common Prayer. This service may be used with or without

the eucharist and may include baptisms. Preparation, therefore, depends upon the type of service accompanying it. The
color may be that of the season of the Church year, but the
best use is generally thought to be white.

CELEBRATION OF A NEW MINISTRY

The instituting and inducting of a priest as rector of a parish
is done by the bishop of the diocese, or his representative,
using the Prayer Book rite. The bishop, when present, is the
chief celebrant of the eucharist. In his absence, the priest
being inducted is the chief celebrant.

The vestments for the rector-elect will be those customarily
worn in the parish. White is the preferred color.

Since this is a festive occasion, the service is usually followed by a reception in the parish house.

COMMUNION OF THE SICK

A small case should be provided for the clergy who carry the
Holy Communion to the sick. It should contain a small,
standing cross or crucifix, two matching candlesticks with
candles, and a book or box of matches. A corporal or other
white linen cloth with a cross embroidered on it is needed to
place the vessels upon. The priest may use a small communion set or just a pyx.

A white stole and a purificator complete the necessary
equipment. A special white stole made of narrow ribbon (two
inch) with fringed ends might be preferred to the regular
stole.

This case must be checked often and all of its contents kept
clean and cared for.

BLESSING OF VESTMENTS AND VESSELS

New vestments, chalices and patens, and other vessels and
equipment, which are to be blessed before use, may be placed
upon the altar before a service. Vestments should be neatly
folded and should be removed by an acolyte or server immediately after they are blessed.

Vestments may also be blessed in the sacristy and this is

sometimes planned when a visit by the bishop is imminent.

According to ancient canon law, certain things are traditionally reserved for the bishop to bless. The altar and its appointments and the chalice and paten should be blessed by the diocesan bishop or his representative. Parish priests may bless vestments and ornaments for their own churches or for use elsewhere.

RECONCILIATION OF A PENITENT

Your parish may be one in which confessions have not been heard, but if the practice is started, the members of the Altar Guild will be expected to know what preparations to make.

Confessions may be heard anywhere but if heard in the church the confessor may sit inside the altar rail or in a place set aside to give greater privacy. The penitent kneels nearby. If preferred, the confessor and penitent may sit face to face for a spiritual conference leading to absolution.

When confessions are heard in the church, the clergyman is usually vested in cassock and purple stole. For confessions heard elsewhere, the cassock could be omitted, but not the stole.

There is a special stole sometimes used for confessions, made of narrow purple grosgrain ribbon with fringed ends. This may be worn instead of the regular purple stole.

The equipment needed for the penitent is a kneeling cushion and a Prayer Book, properly marked at page 447.

The priest must have a purple stole, a Prayer Book, and a Bible. A chair should also be provided. If possible, a shelf might be provided for each, to hold these appointments.

7

Equipment and Adornments

*****

FLOWERS

Every sacristy should have a church calendar which gives the proper colors for each Sunday in the Church year, the seasonal colors for every day, and the colors for other commemorations listed in the Prayer Book Calendar. This will indicate what color vestments to use, and the flowers should be chosen to harmonize. Calendars appropriate for the sacristy are *The New Episcopal Church Calendar, The Ashby Church Kalendar, Churchman's Ordo Kalendar*, and others. Ask your priest which to use; not all agree.

All flowers for the altar should be carefully arranged, preferably by members of the Altar Guild. There is an unfortunate trend among the Altar Guilds today to have flowers for the altar arranged by florists. The flowers arranged by members may not have so professional a look—although many women are expert at this—but offering them as a service of love will surely be missed if they are commercially done.

Flowers should not dominate an altar. They are symbols of the Resurrection and their purpose is to add beauty to the setting. They are not a necessary adjunct of the worship service and thus should be subordinate to the cross and candles. Decorators should not be permitted in the sanctuary nor should the sometimes overpowering decorations used at weddings and funerals be allowed.

Generally speaking, white flowers should be used at festivals. On Pentecost, red gladioli are very effective and red flowers are also appropriate at Confirmation. On the Sunday after Easter, sometimes called "Low" Sunday, or the Sunday with the gospel of the Five Wounds glorified, white flowers should be used with the addition of five red flowers, such as carnations, put in each vase. These symbolize the Five Wounds.

Churches which use flowers on their altars during Advent should have purple or violet ones if at all possible. No flowers should be put on altars during Lent (and this includes the Sundays of Lent), except on Maundy Thursday for the special commemoration of the institution of the Holy Communion. At chapel altars where the Blessed Sacrament is reserved, there may at all times be a vase with a few flowers.

When the altar flowers are still fresh after the last Sunday service, it is thoughtful to send them to the parish sick. A suitable card should accompany them with the church's name. Such cards can be obtained from church supply houses. The rector can furnish the names of those to whom he wishes the flowers sent, and a special committee of women who are not members of the Altar Guild might be chosen to deliver them.

If funds are needed to supply flowers for the altar, parishioners could be given the opportunity to contribute them as memorials or as thanksgiving offerings during specified months. This might become a yearly custom for them. An altar flower chart, obtainable at church supply stores, could be posted in the back of the church as a reminder. It should be understood that, except in very special cases, the flowers will be selected and purchased by the Altar Guild, lest the individuals get unsuitable ones, or too many or too few.

A standard fee should be decided upon and charged all donors. A bill is sent them by the Altar Guild treasurer when their Sunday falls due, or on the first of the month thereafter. It is also well to send them a note in advance to advise them of the approach of their day. Some make a special effort to be present at the church services on these occasions.

CANDLES

The only candles necessary upon an altar are the ones used at the celebration of the Holy Communion. Any others are for adornment.

The six "office" lights, three on each side of the cross, very generally used in our churches, are to add to the beauty and symbolism of the sanctuary. When extra candlesticks are added on festival occasions, this is done to make the setting more beautiful, and one must be certain that this end is accomplished or they had better not be used. Balance must be maintained and the altar not look over-dressed.

Candles should be put upon an altar only if they are to be lighted. For instance, at an early celebration of the Holy Communion on Easter and Christmas when there is no music, only the eucharistic candles should be used. If there are later choral services on these festivals, branch candelabra may be added to give a more festive setting. Good taste is the final arbiter since we have no directive by rubric.

The candles on the epistle side are lighted first and extinguished last. The lighting and extinguishing of candles is not part of the worship service itself and should be done as quietly and unobtrusively as possible, generally by the acolytes.

The paschal candle is referred to under the instructions for the Great Vigil of Easter.

It is very helpful, clean, and economical, to have draft guards or caps, sometimes called followers, to put on top of the candles. They keep the melted wax from running down the sides of the candles. This makes for tidiness and saves work, as well as for economy because all the wax is consumed and the candles burn down more slowly. The guards can be bought at church supply houses to fit almost any size candles and come in glass, chrome, or brass. The brass ones are more expensive, heavier, and more conspicuous than glass, but are also more durable. However, with reasonable care the glass ones should last indefinitely.

New candles should be lighted for a moment before being put in use, to be sure they will burn correctly and not go out during a service. If the wicks are too long, they should be trimmed. If too short, a little well dug around them will permit melted wax to drip there and keep the candle burning.

Candles come in a great variety of widths and lengths. They are ordered from supply houses by their brand names and not usually by the uses to which they are put in the church. Width measurements are taken across the bottom of the candle. This measurement is also used when ordering the guards or followers for the tops.

When purchasing candlesticks, it is advisable to get them with large holders if possible. Thicker and taller candles, which look better and last for a longer time, may then be used.

When altar candles burn down too low to look well, the stubs may be used in torches or on church school altars or side altars. When too short even for this, they may be collected in lots of forty or fifty pounds and sold back to the candle companies for a small sum.

VESTMENTS OF THE CLERGY
It is greatly to be desired that there be a priest's sacristy, however small, so that the clergy do not have to vest in the same room used by the Altar Guild when preparing for the services. Nevertheless, many churches have but one sacristy available and when this is the case, the women of the Altar Guild must get their work done early enough to give the priest room and privacy to prepare for the services.

Much ingenuity must frequently be practiced to keep the clergy vestments clean, pressed, and in order in a limited space. However, somehow it must be done. The clergy must not go into the sanctuary in wrinkled surplice or alb. Linen or synthetic vestments should not be worn twice without pressing and should be laundered promptly when they need it.

Vestments necessary for a priest are cassock with cincture, surplice, four stoles in the colors of the Church seasons, and a tippet. The tippet is a black scarf worn in place of the

stole at Morning or Evening Prayer or
other choir offices. Many clergy use
the cassock-alb for celebrations of the
Holy Communion. The number of
surplices and cassock-albs may be
determined by the frequency of
services at which they are worn.

If eucharistic vestments are worn at
celebrations of the Holy Communion,
these should be supplied by the church.
They will be needed in the four colors.
Some churches have black for requiems. They come in sets and vary
greatly in price according to the
materials used. These sets can be
bought from church supply houses if
the Altar Guild boasts no needle-
women sufficiently skilled to make
them.

**A PRIEST IN
CASSOCK (1), SURPLICE (2),
AND STOLE (3)**

Diocesan Altar Guilds are often
glad to take orders for eucharistic
vestments and this might be considered before a commercial
house is contacted.

Special care must be taken of eucharistic vestments. Chasubles may be either hung on padded hangers in a cupboard
or laid flat in drawers, if the drawers are sufficiently large
to permit the minimum of folding. If the bottom of the
chasuble must be folded up, a roll of tissue over a tube should
be put between the folds.

Chasubles are usually made of colored silk damask, or
rayon, or similar materials. They may also be made of white
linen, possibly trimmed with braid in the seasonal colors.
These are welcome in very warm climates or where economy
must be practiced.

The chalice veil should be laid flat when put away:

The alb, amice, and white rope girdle complete the eucharistic vestments. The alb is usually made of linen or cotton,

but silk, rayon, nylon, and other fabrics are also used. Amices may differ a great deal. Today some are part of the alb at the neck while others are rectangular with strings attached. The girdle is a rope of linen or cotton, sometimes rayon, woven or knitted, used to belt the alb at the waist. It has knots or tassels at the ends.

A PRIEST IN
EUCHARISTIC
VESTMENTS

The chasuble is distinctly a eucharistic vestment. It is worn only for a celebration of the Holy Communion. It should not be worn in procession through the church or into the pulpit.

A special alb, which has lace at the hem and on the cuffs, may be provided for festivals. Some priests prefer an "appareled" alb with amice to match. Apparels are oblong pieces of silk damask usually in gold, or red and gold, or blue and gold. They are tacked to the front and to the back of the alb above the hem, and also on the sleeves above the cuffs. A matching apparel fits along the collar of the amice. The Altar Guild attends to tacking the apparels on. They are beautiful and very effective at festivals.

Albs may differ in style, as may amices. Some priests prefer a collarless amice with folds around the neck. Others prefer a soft collar. Still others like a stiff collar and in this case it is better to have the amice made with an opening along the whole back, except at the ends, so that plastic stiffening (sheets or rolls at stationery stores) cut to fit may be inserted. Do not use starch in church linens. An amice made like a monk's hood with a button at the neck is preferred by some priests.

The surplice is a vestment which may be worn by the clergy at any of the Church's services.

The stole is a band of colored silk of slightly varying widths, worn around the neck. It is lined, usually has a small cross embroidered at the neck, and symbols on each end. Of the two stoles most frequently worn, the eucharistic stole differs from the "preaching" stole in length. The eucharistic stole is fifty inches long without the fringe; it is longer in order to show below the chasuble. The preaching stole is about forty inches long without the fringe; its ends hang to the knees.

The color of the stole worn follows the season of the Church year. Small collars of linen or lawn, possibly edged with narrowest lace, may be tacked at the neck of preaching stoles to protect them from wear. These are about twelve inches long and two inches wide, with about a third of their width turned over on the inside. They should be frequently laundered.

A DEACON IN
CASSOCK (1), SURPLICE (2),
AND STOLE (3)

Most priests in time acquire their own stoles, but each church should have a set of its own. They are necessary for rectors who may not have any, as well as for additional, or visiting, clergy.

The stole is always worn when administering any of the sacraments of the Church. The deacon wears the stole over the left shoulder, one end folded over the other. Both priest and bishop wear the stole hanging straight down. Some priests still prefer to cross their eucharistic stoles as was the custom for many years.

As stated in Chapter 6, a purple stole is worn for confessions, or a special stole of narrow purple ribbon about two inches wide. This has fringed ends and a small cross.

The cope is a large and elaborate cloak or cape, usually

richly embroidered, worn at festivals and at other formal services. This is an expensive vestment and often the last one a parish acquires. Copes are sometimes given as memorials. The color most favored for copes is gold since it is suitable at any season. White, blue, red, rose, or variations of these are also used, if the parish does not have a set of copes for all of the seasons of the Christian year. The cope has a shield or hood at the back and is fastened across the breast by a clasp called a morse.

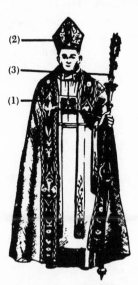

A BISHOP IN COPE (1) AND MITRE (2), WITH PASTORAL STAFF OR CROZIER (3)

The cap of the clergy is called a biretta. It is a black square with a pompom on top. Most birettas can be folded flat for packing. Some clergy wear a soft, flat hat known as the "Canterbury Cap" instead of a biretta.

The bishop's biretta is red. He may also wear a red skull cap called a zuchetto. With the cope a bishop wears a two-pointed, cloven headdress called a mitre.

In cold climates the priest should have a black wool cape to wear over vestments out of doors.

Some ministers wear their academic hoods at Morning Prayer or upon other occasions. This hood is worn over the surplice, around the neck, and hangs down the back. It goes under the tippet and is not worn with the stole. The

A BIRETTA

hood denotes a university degree and is not an ecclesiastical vestment.

LINENS AND SUPPLIES
Every congregation should consider it essential for the church
to have a suitably equipped altar and sanctuary. The number
of linens in the Altar Guild's inventory depends upon the size
of the church and the number of services.

Linens for the altar and sanctuary are:
Cerecloth
Fair linen
Frontal or superfrontal
Prayer cloth to cover the fair linen
Dust protector for altar
Credence table cover
Others according to need

Linens for the Sacraments are:
Purificators
Lavabo towels or mundatorys
Corporals
Chalice veils and burses
Palls and pall protectors
Baptismal towels
Tabernacle linens and hangings (if used)
Others according to parish custom

VESSELS
Certain vessels are necessary adjuncts to worship in the Episcopal Church. If in new missions and under certain condi-
tions in parishes it is unavoidable that substitutes for these be
used, suitable and correct vessels should be procured as soon
as possible. In very many cases these are given to churches as
memorials.

Vessels needed for the Holy Communion are:
Chalice and paten
Bread box
Wine and water cruets
Lavabo bowl

Wine may be kept in the bottle in which it comes from the
manufacturer. It may also be stored in a flagon, or in a large
glass cruet, or in a decanter.

If the sacrament is reserved, a ciborium will be needed as well as a pyx.

When it is the custom of the parish to use incense, a censer, or thurible, with a "boat" will be necessary.

PATEN   CHALICE   LAVABO BOWL   CIBORIUM

Alms basins, or offering plates, must be provided, the number and size depending on parish needs. A large receiving basin for the smaller plates will be helpful.

Vessels needed for baptisms are:

Ewer, usually of silver or brass

Baptismal bowl

Baptismal shell

A small communion set for administering to the sick should be acquired. Some priests have these given them by family or friends at their ordinations, but when it is possible for the parish to have one of its own it is much more satisfactory.

Sacristy supplies include:
  Hand towels for clergy—linen, cotton, or terry cloth
  Covers for vesting chest
  Cleaning and polishing cloths
  Soaps, polishes, and brushes
  Sewing equipment
  Notepads, labels, pencils, tape, thumb tacks
These are but a few needs and each individual Altar Guild
will determine its own. Everything should be done to keep
the altar and sacristy appointments well cared for and any-
thing required to bring this about should be procured.

A Church calendar, which gives the days and colors of the
Church Year, as well as other pertinent information, is a necessity in every sacristy (see Chapter 7, under "Flowers"). If
the parish has a daily or even one week-day celebration of the
Holy Communion, a calendar which gives the official days
for saints, martyrs, and lesser church figures is helpful. Its use
would depend upon the direction of the rector.

NOTES ON LINENS
Linens used in the service of the altar should be handled with
care, especially in the laundering. Unless the church has a
washing machine and laundry equipment, church linens are
laundered in the homes of Altar Guild members. This work
should be given priority and the linens returned promptly to
the sacristy—certainly within the week. Most churches do not
have an abundant supply and will be inconvenienced if the
stock gets low.

Synthetic materials are now coming into use but linen is
still favored as by far the best fabric for church use. Wine and
lipstick are the most troublesome stains. Both can be removed
after soaking in a warm soap solution. If purificators stained
with lipstick are then re-soaped and the stains gently rubbed
between the thumb and finger they will generally disappear.
If they persist, soak them in water with a few drops of
bleach. This may have to be done with wine stains as well—
especially where red wine is used. If wine stains are not prop-

erly removed, when the linen is ironed they will reappear as dark smudges.

Purificators and corporals should be ironed from the center out, folded in perfect thirds, and pressed gently with the hands, not mashed flat with the iron. This ironing directive applies to lavabo towels and amices as well. Corporals should be folded wrong side out to be more easily spread upon the Altar. Linens put on rolls should also be wrong side out. When linens are put on rolls, white tissue should be put around them with a label to identify them. The tissue when folded at the ends will hold the linen on the roll. Scotch tape should not be used because it leaves a sticky spot when removed and a stain on the linen when washed.

The ciborium should be covered with a soft white veil with a narrow lace edge. It should have an opening in the top with a button-hole stitch around it for the cross to come through.

Lavabo towels and baptismal towels are very similar. A shell embroidered on the baptismal towel instead of the customary cross will make it easy to distinguish between them.

Wax spots can be removed by placing a blotter under the linen, a piece of brown paper over the spot, and using a hot iron. A blob of wax, after it is firmly set, may be taken off by careful scraping with a knife. The above hot iron treatment is applied if a spot is left. Wax may be set by rubbing with an ice cube.

High percentage beeswax candles make stubborn stains which may require boiling water repeatedly poured through the stretched linen. Even a mild solvent might have to be used.

It is helpful if the sacristy has an inventory book in which members may list the linens they are taking home to launder. When returned this should be noted so that all linens may be accounted for at all times.

Old linens no longer usable should be carefully burned. Usable ones may be donated to needy missions, possibly through the Diocesan Altar Guild.

8

General Working Policy

* * * * *

Martha said quietly, "The Teacher is here and is calling for thee." When Mary heard this she arose quickly and went to Him. —John 11:28–29

THE ALTAR GUILD

We are the ones chosen to prepare for the meeting of the people with God. Every parish and mission should have a group of women sufficiently devoted to Christ and His Church to give of themselves to the service of the altar. There is no greater privilege for a laywoman in the Church, and only women who appreciate this fact should be chosen to serve. These women must be communicants of the Episcopal Church and, when accepting membership in an Altar Guild, should be willing to make sacrifices of their time usually beyond anything offered the church before. The work should take precedence over ordinary worldly considerations— personal, social, or family.

Care should be taken in the training of the women chosen and their obligation to be present at required and expected times stressed. The Altar Guild is in no sense a social guild. No novice should be admitted to full membership without a period of working probation. The probationary period should last at least six months, and in busier parishes a year is better. This interim will enable the prospective Altar Guild member to determine her feeling for the work and the Guild her suitability to continue. When accepted for full membership, she should be instituted (possibly with other probationers) at a corporate communion of the Guild.

The Altar Guild should have a stated meeting once a month, presided over by its chairman or directress. A secretary is also necessary, as well as a treasurer. If the church is large and active, chairmen in charge of various phases of the work may be helpful, such as sewing, weddings, flowers, supplies, etc. All of these women work harmoniously together under the presiding chairman and make reports to the Guild when called upon to do so. When circumstances arise which prevent attendance at meetings, the chairman should be notified. If any member is unable to fulfill her term of duty, the chairman should be informed so that some other member may substitute for her.

It is desirable that the rector open the meetings with prayer and then present any instructions or changes to be carried out. The rector should not be expected to remain throughout the meeting. If the rector or assistant is unable to be present, the presiding chairman should open the meeting with prayer. An instruction period is extremely helpful at each meeting, perhaps taking up one phase of the work each month. If thus taught, all members learn to perform their duties in a prescribed way.

Meetings of the Altar Guild should take place at the church, if at all possible, and not at the homes of the members as do the social guilds. It is an excellent practice to do the sewing and mending of altar linens during the meetings, and therefore convenience to the sacristy is important.

The matter of paying dues can be settled by each individual Guild. The system adopted for alloting the work depends upon the need of the particular church and the number of its services. There is merit in two members being assigned to work at the same time. It is more pleasant and efficient, and if one is ill the other can make an easy adjustment. Five groups or teams working two weeks at a time (some prefer a month) should be the maximum number for a large parish.

More women may be added, as needed, to the existing teams
rather than to create new teams. Too much time should not
elapse between terms of duty, as would be the case if there
were more groups. One is apt to lose touch and forget details.

It is much more interesting if each member is trained to do
all aspects of the work and is not just a specialist in one phase,
such as flower arrangement or brass polishing.

The Altar Guild chairman should prepare a schedule each
week listing the number, kind, and time of the services. The
list should also include any other information necessary for
the guidance of the workers on duty. The schedule should be
posted in the sacristy.

A member of the Altar Guild should be on duty *and
present* at every public service of the church. There are many
occasions when she may be useful. A celebration of the Holy
Communion cannot take place unless at least one person is
present besides the minister. Two members of the Guild
should be present at every formal wedding.

Many Altar Guild members feel that it is a definite advan-
tage to wear some sort of uniform while working in the sacristy and sanctuary, rather than everyday clothes. The
simplest garment is a smock in brown, or church blue, with a
veil, or cap, to match. If each member does not wish to provide her own, the Guild might make two or more in different
sizes and keep them in the sacristy.

The Altar Guild of every parish would do well to become a
member of the Diocesan Altar Guild and to co-operate with
it whenever possible. To get the feeling that we are all part of
one harmonious whole is an excellent thing, both in this as
well as in other phases of the Church's life. It would be a fine
thing if Diocesan Altar Guilds could have one woman, or a
group of women, trained to go about the Diocese giving instructions in the care and vesting of the Church's altars. New
mission stations are expecially in need of this help, and often
women of older parishes who have not had sufficient training
would also welcome it.

It is the responsibility of every communicant to see to it

that our altars are properly equipped and adequate sacristy facilities are provided. Ideally, there should be two sacristies—one for clergy, one for the Altar Guild.

PERSONNEL

Altar Guild work is a vocation. It is not just another church job, and any woman who has this attitude toward it should direct her talents elsewhere. It differs entirely from work in the social guilds of the Church and a feeling of dedication and self-effacement is essential for any woman aspiring to the privilege of serving at God's altar.

When a new parish or mission is formed, it is fortunate if it has among its members a woman trained in Altar Guild work, who has also a real love for, and knowledge of, the Church and can impart this to others. Lacking any trained women, many churches are at a loss as to how to begin their Altar Guild work. In this case it might be well to ask the loan of a instructor from a neighboring parish, or perhaps the Diocesan Altar Guild might be in a position to provide one. For the most part, priests have had little or no training in this work and although they may have served as sacristan at their seminary, it has not been necessary for them to know many of the details.

When coming into a parish, a priest can usually give instructions about the results wanted, expecting that the Altar Guild women know how to bring them about. The rector of a parish sets the pattern for its ceremonial. When there is a change, the Altar Guild should have sufficient training to follow a new lead. It is sometimes a time of stress, but the Guild exists to carry out the rector's orders and should do so with the same cheerful willingness always. Members should not let their personal feelings or opinions intrude. The inspiration for service which unites them all must govern their actions so that everything will be done "decently and in order."

One of the chief reasons why devoted Altar Guild members are few and hard to find is that many do not love the Church enough to make sacrifices for it. Worldly considerations are allowed to supplant the Church, and putting the service at the altar ahead of other desires is an inconvenience and a discipline to which they will not submit. Doing the work half-heartedly and in haste to get off to something else does not indicate the proper feeling for it and the results will show it. Working in the church's sanctuary is a wonderful release from the pressure of the world and should be balm to the spirit.

Only women who can work harmoniously together should serve on an Altar Guild. Sometimes members of long standing cannot adjust to changes brought about by the coming of a new rector or a new Guild directress. If so, they should resign from the Guild in order that the holy work in which they are all engaged may continue serenely. A large measure of good judgment and sweet temper are priceless attributes in carrying out the duties of a handmaiden in God's house.

Except for essential conversation about the work at hand, silence should be maintained in the sanctuary. Work done in the sacristy and sanctuary should begin and end with prayer.

ACOLYTES

The training of acolytes should be the prerogative of the priest, since acolytes perform some of the most important functions in the Church. Many of the clergy are recruited from the ranks of our acolytes and the importance of their instruction cannot be over stressed. Thus, although acolyte training is not usually included in the duties of Altar Guild members, nevertheless there are a good many occasions when only the Altar Guild worker and the acolyte are present before a service. The acolyte may be new and in need of help. It seems wise, therefore, for Altar Guild women to have a general knowledge of correct procedure for acolytes.

Acolytes must not go into the sanctuary unless fully vested in cassock and cotta. They must not light or extinguish candles while vested in cassock only. In lighting candles, those on the epistle side are lighted first and extinguished last. Those nearest the cross are lighted first and extinguished last. At a choral celebration of the Holy Communion, the eucharistic candles are lighted first, before the "office" lights. At a service where there are two acolytes, they may light the candles together, one on each side, beginning with the candles nearest the cross. They are extinguished in reverse order. When the acolytes come to the altar to light the candles they bow to the cross. It is not necessary for them to do so again until they have finished their work and are ready to withdraw. Crucifers and torch-bearers do not bow while carrying these symbols. They face the altar when arriving there in procession and again upon leaving. Candles should be lighted and extinguished with the minimum of ceremony. It is not a part of the service itself. The service is ended when the clergy leave the church, not when the candles are extinguished.

When the sacrament is reserved at the altar, it is customary to genuflect before it. Acolytes lighting candles genuflect when they come to the altar and again upon leaving. Crucifiers and torch-bearers, because they are carrying these symbols, do not genuflect or bow. Other acolytes genuflect before the sacrament.

Churches which vest their acolytes in red cassocks might provide black ones for the penitential seasons of Advent and Lent. Black may be worn at burials and requiems. Clergy and acolytes serving at some cathedrals wear purple cassocks. In warm climates, many churches vest both choirs and acolytes in white cassocks.

The proper vestments for acolytes are cassocks and cottas. Some churches have adopted the practice of vesting their crucifers and servers in albs for celebrations of the Holy Eucharist or at high festivals.

FEES

Strictly speaking, fees for the Church's services are not the concern of the Altar Guild. Inquiries about them should be referred to the rector.

The Episcopal Church does not charge for the sacraments.

However, the administration of the sacraments requires material agents, all of which cost money. Our churches must be heated and lighted. Repairs must be made and employees paid. For the most part, churches are maintained by the regular offerings of faithful communicants and it seems reasonable that persons who use the ministrations of the church for occasional convenience should compensate the church therefor. It is a human attribute to value things for which we must pay. Therefore, when Altar Guild members are consulted about fees by occasional users of the church's facilities, it is a good opportunity to get in a little missionary work and encourage these impulses offering financial aid.

OFFICE OF ADMISSION INTO AN ALTAR GUILD*
This service should always take place at a celebration of the Holy Eucharist, when the Altar Guild is making a corporate communion.

Immediately following the Creed and homily, the chairman of the Altar Guild and the candidates for admission should come forward to the altar rail. With the congregation being seated, the celebrant says these or similar words:

Brothers and Sisters in Christ Jesus, we are all baptized by the one Spirit into one Body, and given gifts for a variety of ministries for the common good. Our purpose is to commission these persons in the Name of God and of this congregation to a special ministry to which they are called.

Are these persons you are to present prepared by a commitment to Christ as Lord, by regular attendance at worship, and by the knowledge of their duties, to exercise their ministry to the honor of God, and the well-being of His Church?

Chairman: I believe that they are.

Celebrant: You have been called to a ministry in this congregation. Will you, as long as you are engaged in this work, perform it with diligence?

Candidates: I will.

*From The Book of Occasional Services, ©1979 Church Pension Fund. Used by Permission.

Celebrant: Will you faithfully and reverently execute the duties of your ministry to the honor of God, and the benefit of the members of this congregation?

Candidates: I will.

Chairman: I present to you these persons to be admitted to the ministry of the Altar Guild in this congregation.

Celebrant: The Levites were responsible for the ark, the table, the lampstand, the altars, and the vessels of the sanctuary with which the priests minister. In the temple of the Lord all are crying, "Glory!"

Response: Holiness adorns your house, O Lord, for ever.

Celebrant: Let us pray.

O Lord, Jesus Christ, who did accept the ministry of faithful women during your earthly life, we pray you to accept and bless the work which these women are about to undertake in the care of your sanctuary. Grant them a spirit of reverence for your house and worship, your Word and holy Sacraments, and preserve in purity and holiness their souls and bodies as living temples of your Presence, to whom, with the Father and the Holy Spirit, we give praise and honor, now and forever. Amen.

In the name of God and of this congregation, I commission you [N.] as a member of the Altar Guild of this Parish [and give you this _____ as a token of your ministry].

*****

Mimeographed copies of this service may be made and passed out to the candidates. The copies could be collected afterwards and kept for future use.

Blessed are those servants whom the Lord when he cometh shall find watching.—Luke 12:37

9

Definitions of Church Terms

*****

Ablutions—Ceremonial cleansing of the chalice and paten by the celebrant after the Holy Communion.

Academic Hood—A hood worn over the shoulders and down the back, denoting a college degree. It has no ecclesiastical significance.

Acolyte—One who attends or serves the priest in the sanctuary.

Alb—A white, sleeved garment which covers the entire cassock. It is worn by the sacred ministers at Holy Communion as part of the eucharistic vestments.

Alms Basin also spelled *Bason*—A large circular vessel of greater width than depth, usually made of wood, brass, or silver, in which are placed the offerings of the congregation.

Altar—The holy table upon which the Holy Communion is celebrated.

Altar Bread—The wafers or bread used at the Holy Communion.

Altar Cloth—See *Frontal* and *Superfrontal*.

Ambulatory—A passageway, or corridor, behind an altar.

Amice—A large square, or oblong, of white linen or cotton. It is worn about the shoulders, over the cassock. The upper part is first placed over the head that it may fall like a collar over the alb. It is tied with crossed strings around the waist.

Ampulla—A cruet for wine or water.

Ante-Communion—The part of the communion service which precedes the oblations; also known as "The Liturgy of the Word."

Antependium—A hanging before the altar, or for the pulpit or lectern; a frontal.

Apparels—Oblong pieces of colored silk or brocade, tacked above the hem on the front, back, and sleeves of the alb, as well as on the collar of the amice.

Aumbry—A closed niche in the sanctuary wall used from ancient times for reservation of the sacrament or for the holy oils.

Baptistry or *Baptistery*—The place where the font is located, usually near the entrance of church.

Bier lights—Tall candlesticks which stand on the nave floor at the chancel steps beside a coffin. There may be two, one on each side, or as many as six, three on each side.

Biretta—A stiff, four-sided cap worn by the clergy. A priest or deacon wears black, a bishop purple or red.

Bishop—The highest order of the sacred ordained ministry in the Episcopal Church; the head of a diocese, elected by the diocese.

Bishop Coadjutor—A bishop elected and given jurisdiction to assist and later to succeed the diocesan bishop.

Bishop, Presiding—The Chief Pastor and Primate of The Episcopal Church, elected by the House of Bishops and confirmed by the House of Deputies. Serves a term of twelve years.

Bishop, Suffragan—A bishop elected to assist the diocesan bishop, but without jurisdiction or right of succession.

Bishop's Chair—A special chair on the gospel side of the sanctuary, reserved for the diocesan bishop on his visitations.

Bread Box—A box, usually of silver, in which is kept the bread or wafers for the Holy Communion.

Burse—A square case used to hold the corporal, the post-communion veil, and the purificators at the Holy Communion.

Cassock—A long, closely fitting garment reaching from the neck to the shoe tops, worn by clergy, acolytes, and choir. It may be worn for every official occasion. A priest wears black, a bishop purple or red.

Catechist—A lay person trained, examined, and specifically licensed by the diocesan bishop to teach within a parish.

Celebrant—The priest who celebrates the Holy Communion.

Celebration—The consecration and administration of the Holy Communion.

Censer—A swinging vessel on a chain, used for burning incense.

Cerecloth—The first, waxed linen cloth upon the altar.

Chalice—The cup used for the wine at the Holy Communion.

Chalice Veil—See *Post-Communion Veil* and *Silk Chalice Veil*.

Chancel—The east end of the church, raised above the floor of the nave, containing the choir (usually) and the sanctuary.

Chasuble—The chief eucharistic vestment. It is oval in shape, made without sleeves and has an opening for the head.

Chimere—A long garment with arm holes, but without sleeves. It is worn by a bishop over the rochet and may be either black or red.

Choir—The choristers; also the part of the chancel between the nave and the sanctuary, where the daily offices are said.

Choir Office—A service said in the choir instead of in the sanctuary, such as Morning and Evening Prayers.

Chrism—A consecrated oil used for ceremonial anointing.

Ciborium—A chalice-like cup with a cover, used for the bread at the Holy Communion. Also used to hold the reserved sacrament.

Cincture—A wide, flat, cloth belt or girdle worn around the cassock.

Clergy—Those in Holy Orders: bishops, priests, and deacons.

Compline—A special evening service, the last service of the day.

Cope—A long elaborate cloak of colored silk or brocade worn by a bishop or priest at processions on festival occasions. It has a clasp at the neck called a morse.

Corbel—Small shelves fashioned to the wall on each side of the altar to hold flowers.

Corporal—A square cloth of white linen. The sacred vessels are placed upon it at a celebration of the Holy Communion.

Cotta—A white garment similar to a surplice, but shorter and without a cross on the front. Worn by choir and acolytes over the cassock.

Credence—A shelf or table upon which the cruets, bread box, lavabo bowl, lavabo towel, and extra chalices are placed in readiness for the Holy Communion.

Crozier—A bishop's pastoral staff.

Crucifer—The cross-bearer in a procession.

Cruet—A vessel holding wine or water used at the Holy Communion.

Crucifix—The cross with the figure of our Lord upon it.

Dalmatic—The colored silk eucharistic vestment worn by the deacon at a solemn celebration of the Holy Communion.

Deacon—The first of the three orders of the ordained ministry.

Deacon's Step—The second of the three steps approaching the altar.

Dean—The chief of the clergy on the staff of a cathedral; also the clerical head of a seminary; also a parish priest appointed by the bishop to be his representative in a specific area of the diocese.

Diocese—The see or jurisdiction of a bishop.

Dossal—A tapestry or curtain which hangs behind the altar.

Elements—The bread, wine, and water which are used at the Holy Communion.

Epistle Side—The right side of the sanctuary as one faces the altar.

Eucharist—One of the most ancient names for the Holy Communion; comes from the Greek meaning "thanksgiving."

Eucharistic Ministers—Persons specifically licensed by the diocesan bishop to administer the cup at any celebration of the Holy Communion if there is an insufficient number of priests or deacons present; and, in some dioceses, may take the consecrated sacrament to the sick and shut-ins of the parish.

Eucharistic Vestments—The special vestments worn at a celebration of the Holy Communion: alb, amice, girdle, stole, chasuble, and maniple.

Ewer—The container holding the baptismal water at the font.

Fair linen—The principal white linen cloth covering the altar, required by rubric.

Flagon—A vessel to hold the reserve of wine at the Holy Communion.

Font—The bowl of stone, marble, or metal, on a pedestal, in which the water for Holy Baptism is blessed.

Footpace—The platform upon which the altar rests; the top step before the altar.

Frontal—A covering which hangs over the front of the altar, reaching to the floor.

Frontlet—A superfrontal, or short cover, which hangs in front of the altar; used over the frontal, if there be one.

Girdle—A white rope of linen or cotton worn about the waist over the alb. Black girdles are sometimes worn over the cassock.

Gospel Side—The left side of the sanctuary as one faces the altar.

Gradine—A retable; the shelf behind the altar.

Holy Mysteries—An ancient term used for the Holy Communion.

Hood—The short cape or shield at the back of the cope. See also *Academic Hood*.

Host—The consecrated bread or wafer at the Holy Communion. The priest's host is larger than the wafers used to communicate the people.

IHS—The Sacred Monogram. The first three letters of the name JESUS in Greek.

Incense—A mixture of spices for ceremonial burning, symbolizing prayer.

Lavabo Bowl—A small bowl for water used by the celebrant at the Holy Communion to wash his fingers.

Lavabo Towel—The small towel which is used with the lavabo bowl.

Lay Reader—A lay person especially licensed by the bishop to hold certain Prayer Book services for a specific diocesan congregation. May also include a license to preach.

Lectern—A stand at the chancel rail upon which the Bible rests.

Lector—A lay person who reads from Holy Scripture at either the Holy Communion or one of the choir offices. May not read the gospel at the eucharist.

Maniple—A short band worn on the left arm by some celebrants at Holy Communion as part of the eucharistic vestments.

Mass—One of the names for the Holy Mysteries; the Holy Communion.

Mensa—The top of the altar, or holy table.

Missal—The altar service book, containing the service of the Holy Communion.

Missal Stand—The stand or desk upon which the altar service book rests.

Mitre—The headdress of a bishop: two-pointed and cloven, worn with the cope or eucharistic vestments. It symbolizes the "tongues of fire" at the descent of the Holy Spirit upon the apostles at Pentecost.

Morse—The clasp at the neck of the cope, sometimes jewelled.

Mundatory—A lavabo towel.

Nave—The body of a church building, where the congregation worships.

Oblations—The bread and wine offered for consecration at the eucharist.

Offertory—The offering of the bread and wine and alms at the Holy Communion.

Office—A service of the church, other than the Holy Communion, such as Morning and Evening Prayer.

Ordination—The conferring of Holy Orders by a bishop.

Orphrey—An embroidered band on a chasuble or other vestment or hanging.

Pall—A square of aluminum, cardboard, or plastic, covered with linen, placed over the chalice.

Pall, Funeral—A large silk or brocade cover for a coffin.

Paschal Candle—A large candle which stands on the floor of the sanctuary on the gospel side from the Great Vigil of Easter until the Ascension Day. It symbolizes our Lord's Resurrection; may also be used at baptisms throughout the year.

Paten—The plate for the bread used at the Holy Communion.

Pectoral Cross—The large cross worn by a bishop.

Pentecost—The Sunday fifty days after Easter which commemorates the receiving of the gifts of the Holy Spirit by the apostles; celebrated as the birthday of the Church.

Piscina—A basin with a drain directly to the ground where water used in the sacrament of Holy Baptism is poured; or where the first water used in cleansing the vessels and linens of the Holy Communion is poured.

Post-Communion Veil—A fine linen or lawn veil used to cover the chalice after the Holy Communion if the ablutions are not taken immediately after the communions; sometimes called a chalice veil.

Prayer Cloth—A white linen cloth which covers the top of the altar, over the fair linen, for all services except the Holy Communion.

Predella—The Footpace.

Priest—The second of the three orders of the ordained ministry; one who has been ordained by a bishop to administer the sacraments of the Church.

Protector—A cloth used to cover the altar, between services, to protect it from dust.

Purificator—A small square of linen with a cross upon it, used by the celebrant to cleanse the chalice and paten after the Holy Communion.

Pyx —A small receptacle, like a watch case, used to carry the reserved sacrament to the sick.

Rector—A priest who is the head of a parish.

Reredos—The panel of wood or stone behind the altar.

Retable—A shelf at the back of the altar (pronounced ré-table); also called a gradine.

Riddels—Curtains hung at each side of an altar.

Rochet—A long white linen vestment with wide sleeves tied at the wrists, worn by a bishop under the chimere. It may have lace at the hem and on the cuffs. It generally is worn under a cope or on occasions when the bishop does not wear the chimere. A bishop may also wear a short rochet with close fitting sleeves like an alb.

Rood—A cross or crucifix.

Rood Beam—A beam between the nave and the chancel with the rood upon it.

Rood Screen—A screen separating the nave from the chancel and having the rood upon it.

Rubric—A rule or direction in the Book of Common Prayer governing the conduct of services.

Sacristan—One in charge of the sacristy.

Sacristy—The place or room in which the sacred vessels, linens, and vestments are kept.

Sedilia—The seats, within the sanctuary, for the clergy and acolytes.

See—The diocese of a bishop.

Server—An acolyte.

Silk Chalice Veil—A square covering of silk or brocade, used to cover the chalice and paten before and after the service of Holy Communion.

Stole—A long, narrow band of silk worn over the shoulders of the clergy. It is worn over the surplice or alb and is the color of the day.

Subdeacon—The minister who reads the epistle at a solemn celebration of the Holy Communion, whether he is a bishop, priest, deacon, or layman.

Subdeacon's Step—The first of the three altar steps.

Superfrontal—A short hanging for the front of the altar. It may be used over a frontal or separately and be made of lace or of colored silk.

Surplice—A white vestment with full flowing sleeves. It is longer than a cotta and normally has a cross on the front.

Tabernacle—A closed compartment at the back of the altar used to house the reserved sacrament.

Thurible—The vessel which holds the burning incense. It swings on a chain. The "boat" is the metal container in which the incense is reserved.

Thurifer—The one who swings the censer containing the burning incense.

Tippet—A black scarf, wider than a stole, worn about the neck, with ends hanging down in front. It is worn by the clergy at choir offices.

Tunicle—The colored silk eucharistic vestment worn by the subdeacon at a solemn celebration of the Holy Communion.

Use—A term meaning the way things are done.

Verger—In some parishes, the individual who takes care of the interior fabric of the church; also sexton.

Vicar—A priest in charge of a mission or chapel.

Vigil—The eve of a feast; a fast before a feast and a watch, as before the Blessed Sacrament on Maundy Thursday.

Wafer—The unleavened bread used at the Holy Communion.

Zuchetto—The skull cap worn by a bishop. If worn by a priest it is black.

guide back

square

Corporal

outside on top

(~~the~~ backside on

bottom — folded

into 3rds. twice

sm. ~~square~~

purificator

backside on top

folded into 3rds.

twice

oblong — lava bowl

towel

3rds (sort of) &

then in half —